PHYSICS PROJECTS FOR YOUNG SCIENTISTS

PHYSICS PROJECTS FOR YOUNG SCIENTISTS

Revised Edition

Richard C. Adams
and
Peter H. Goodwin

FRANKLIN WATTS
A Division of Grolier Publishing
New York ▪ London ▪ Hong Kong ▪ Sydney
Danbury, Connecticut

NOTE TO READERS:

In this book, some measurements are given only in metric or in English units. There are two reasons for this. In some cases, materials and equipment are sold according to either metric or English measurements. In other cases, it is important for you to know a measurement's value precisely. A degree of accuracy is lost when a converted measurement is rounded to the nearest significant figure.

Photographs ©: Archive Photos: 19; Courtesy of Patricia C. Wright: 79; Envision: 67 (David Bishop); Fundamental Photos: cover, 84 (Richard Megna); Monkmeyer Press: 74 (R. Das), 10 (Lew Merrim); Nance S. Trueworthy: 99; Peter Arnold Inc.: 60 (Richard Choy); Photo Researchers: 53 (Fritz Henle), 91 (Chester Higgins Jr.), 12 (Renee Lynn), 32 (Michael Murphy), 87 (Harry Rogers), 41 (Lee F. Snyder), 103 (M. E. Warren); PhotoEdit: 57 (Davis Barber), 52 (Myrleen Ferguson), 24 (Michael Newman), 34 (D. Young-Wolf); Randy Matusow: 111.

Illustrations by Bob Italiano

Visit Franklin Watts on the Internet at:
http://publishing.grolier.com

Library of Congress Cataloging-in-Publication Data

Adams, Richard C.
Physics projects for young scientists—Rev. Ed. / Richard C. Adams and Peter H. Goodwin.
   p.   cm. — (Projects for young scientists)
Rev. ed. of: Physics projects for young scientists / Peter H. Goodwin, (1991.
Includes bibliographical references and index.
Summary: Gives instructions for and explains the principles behind a variety of simple physics experiments.
   ISBN 0-531-11667-0 (lib. bdg.)   0-531-16461-6 (pbk.)
   1. Physics—Experiments—Juvenile literature.   2. Physics—Experiments—Methodology—Juvenile literature.   [1. Physics—Experiments. 2. Experiments.]
I. Adams, Richard C. (Richard Crittenden)   II. Goodwin, Peter, 1951– Physics projects for young scientists.   III. Series.
QC33.P48   1999
530'.078—dc21   98-40401
                                                        CIP

©1991, 2000 Franklin Watts, A Division of Grolier Publishing
All rights reserved. Published simultaneously in Canada.
GROLIER Printed in the United States of America.
PUBLISHING   4 5 6 7 8 9 10 R 09 08 07 06 07 05 04 03 02 01

PHYSICS PROJECTS FOR YOUNG SCIENTISTS

C O N T E N T S

PHYSICS PROJECTS FOR YOUNG SCIENTISTS

This boy may not realize it, but he is learning physics.

CHAPTER

GETTING STARTED

Physics is the study of how matter and energy interact. Because everything in the universe is either matter or energy, you could say that physics is the study of everything. Actually, though, physicists don't study everything. What they do study is how objects behave under various conditions. Some of these objects are smaller than atoms, while others are as large as galaxies.

The word "physics" scares many people, even though we have all studied it since we were babies. Babies explore the world by performing simple experiments. As they shake a rattle, they add some energy to matter and, thereby, produce noise. Noise is a type of energy. As children grow, they conduct more complex experiments. By building towers of blocks and then knocking them down, children learn about gravity and other physical principles.

You use physics every day, too. When you ride a bike or use in-line skates, you must maintain your balance, or

If this girl does not maintain her
center of gravity, she will fall.

center of gravity. If you don't, you will fall down. You know this is true even if you've never heard the term "center of gravity" before. Physics is really just an explanation of the *forces*, energy, and motion you experience every day.

By now you should realize that you don't need to know all the big, fancy words physicists use to do and understand simple physics experiments. However, as your observations and experiments become increasingly involved, more precise words may help you describe what you see more clearly. Knowing more about physics also allows you to investigate things more quickly and may help you reach better conclusions.

Some physics experiments require you to use numbers. Math is a tool that scientists use to understand the physical world. It is not required for all experiments, and you can draw good conclusions from experiments even if you are not a math whiz. Only a few of the projects in this book require more than basic math. If you need help in this area, talk to a math or physics teacher.

As you do the projects, keep in mind that they won't always work the first time you try them. When this happens, think about what might have gone wrong. A single, careless mistake sometimes leads to large problems. Keep in mind that you can learn a great deal from your mistakes. Sometimes they can even lead to unexpected discoveries.

This book will help you approach scientific investigations in the proper way. It will help you ask the right questions and get you started with basic experiments. Each chapter contains a variety of related projects with background material to help you understand the experiments. After you have completed a project, this book will help you draw conclusions from your data.

Some of the basic experiments can be done quickly and are suitable for a classroom science project. Others take more time, so you may have to work on them during weekends or vacations. Although the basic investigations probably aren't original enough for you to enter them in a large science fair, some of the projects described in the Doing More sections would be appropriate. To learn more about designing and carrying out a science fair project, read Appendix 1 at the back of this book.

Now that you know what you will find in this book, it's time to start performing experiments. Don't forget to enjoy your investigations. Some people like doing experiments so much that they become professional scientists and spend their entire lives doing them.

CHAPTER 2

WORKING
SCIENTIFICALLY

Although scientists work in different ways on different problems, they always use the same process. This process is called the *scientific method*. It involves asking questions, developing a *hypothesis*, gathering data, and then trying to answer the questions. This is similar to the way that most people go about solving a problem.

If you say, "Can I afford to buy a bicycle?" and then say, "I think I can," you are forming a hypothesis. You then collect data to see if it really is possible for you to buy one. You think about how much money you can spend and check the prices of the bicycles that interest you. The more data you collect, the more sure you will be about your conclusion. Eventually, you will know whether you can afford to buy a bicycle.

Scientists follow a similar process. A scientist might say, "Gee, I wonder if this ball will bounce higher on a cement floor or on the grass?" The scientist's hypothesis might be: "I think the ball will bounce higher on cement." This is a guess that the scientist might try to prove or disprove with an experiment that involves collecting data. First, the scientist would drop the ball on a cement floor from a specific height and measure the height of its bounce. Next, the scientist would drop the same ball from the same height onto the lawn. After comparing the data, the scientist would know whether the hypothesis was correct.

The scientist would have to be careful to make sure that the data is valid. If the scientist dropped the ball onto cement from a height of 0.5 meter (m) and onto the lawn from a height of 2 m, the results of the experiment would not be accurate. To get accurate results, only one thing, or variable, can change. Since the scientist is interested in how the surface (cement vs. lawn) affects a ball's ability to bounce, he or she must drop the ball from the same height. The scientist must also use the same ball. Changing the size or mass of the ball will not produce accurate results. You should keep this in mind as you carry out the projects in this book.

As you conduct experiments, make careful measurements and record the data in a notebook. That way all your results will be together in one place. Make sure you write down the date and time you perform each experiment. Some scientists and inventors have been awarded patents worth a lot of money because their lab notebooks had dates proving when they had done an important experiment.

Using a word processing program on a computer can make converting your notes into a report easier. Many "all-in-one" programs, such as *ClarisWorks* (now *AppleWorks*) or *Microsoft Works*, allow you to perform calculations as soon as you enter data into a spreadsheet. Spreadsheets can help you keep data neat and allow you to graph numbers as you get them.

If the data collected by conducting a careful experiment supports your hypothesis, then your hypothesis may be true. On the other hand, your data may show that your hypothesis was incorrect. If that happens, don't worry. Even Albert Einstein—one of the greatest physicists who ever lived—made incorrect hypotheses.

CHAPTER 3

THE STUDY
OF
MECHANICS

The study of forces and motion is called *mechanics*. Sir Isaac Newton was the first person to understand the mathematical relationship between the motion of an object and the amount of force exerted on that object. His famous equation $f = ma$ shows that the force, f, exerted on an object of *mass, m*, is related to its *acceleration, a*. A force is a push or pull; all objects have mass that resists a change in motion; acceleration shows how an object's motion changes over time.

Does this equation seem confusing? Here's a real life example to help make it clearer. Suppose you and your mom are riding in a car. Your mom sees a stop sign and presses the brake to stop the car. When the coast is clear, your mom pushes on the accelerator pedal. The engine creates a force, and the car (which has mass) starts to move. Because the car was stationary and then started to move, it accelerated or changed its motion.

Sir Isaac Newton

The motion of other objects can also change when a force is exerted on them. If you hit a ball with a bat, the ball's motion changes. Because the ball exerts a force on the bat, the bat also changes its motion.

A LOOK AT FRICTION

There are many types of forces. One of the forces you encounter every day is *friction*. Friction resists the motion between two objects or surfaces. Cars need friction to start, stop, and go around corners. But too much friction in the engine or other moving parts makes the car stop running. Similarly, throwing sand on ice increases friction between the tires and the ice. However, throwing sand on dry pavement decreases friction between the tires and the road.

Friction occurs when the molecules in two objects interlock as they come into contact. To understand this idea, imagine what happens when you rub two pieces of sandpaper together. The grains of sand collide. This is similar to what happens between molecules of all objects when they come into contact. To gain a better understanding of friction, try the following project.

FRICTION ON A RAMP

Tape the protractor to the table as shown in Figure 1 on page 22. Place the board on the table so that the top edge of one end aligns with the hole in the protractor. As you tilt the board, make sure that the top edge stays aligned with the hole in the protractor.

Place the block of wood on the board, and slowly raise the board until the block starts sliding down the ramp. As soon as the block begins to move, look at the protractor. Write down the angle the board makes with the table.

Tape	Block of wood 5 to 7.5 cm on a side
Table or other flat surface	Eraser, plastic CD case, rock, shoe, ice cube
Plastic protractor	
2.5 × 15 cm board, about 45 cm long	Sandpaper, writing paper, water

Repeat the procedure a couple of times. Be sure to orient the block the same way each time. In this way, you can determine the average angle at which the block begins to slide down the ramp.

What do you think will happen if you orient the block differently? Repeat the experiment to test your hypothesis. Was your hypothesis correct? Record your findings in a notebook.

Replace the block of wood with other objects, such as an eraser, a plastic CD case, a rock, a shoe, and an ice cube. Do these objects begin to slide at the same angle as the block of wood? In each case, try to predict the angle of sliding before you test an object. Keep track of your results in your notebook. You should create a data table that lists the type of object and the angle at which sliding begins.

Now see what happens when you change the surface of the ramp. Tape some sandpaper or notebook paper to the ramp, or pour a liquid, such as water, on top of it. *Caution: Use only safe liquids, such as water, salad oil, or milk. Check with an adult to make sure that your materials are safe and won't stain your hands or work area.* Try to predict which materials will make objects

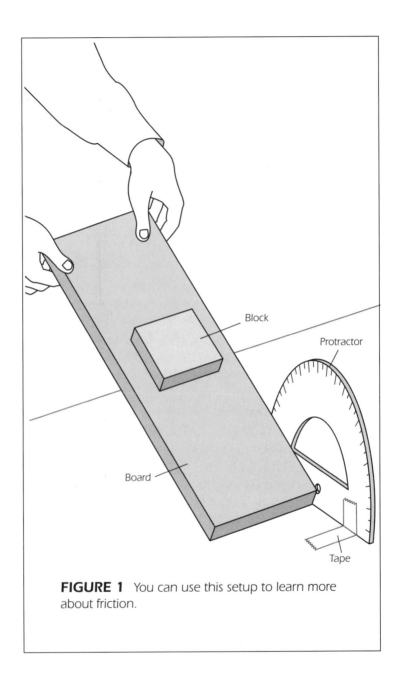

FIGURE 1 You can use this setup to learn more about friction.

slide at smaller angles. After you test each object on each surface material, record your results in a table.

Physicists express the magnitude of friction using a measurement called the *coefficient of friction*—the ratio of the force of friction to the force between the surfaces. The larger the coefficient of friction, the larger the force required to push or pull an object along a surface or, in the case of this experiment, the steeper the ramp must be before the object slides.

When an object slides down a ramp, the coefficient of friction equals the *tangent* of the angle at which an object begins to slide. Tangents can be found using most calculators. If you are unfamiliar with tangents, ask a math or physics teacher to explain them to you. Find the coefficients of friction for the objects you used. Record the values in your data table. Which objects have the largest and the smallest coefficients of friction?

You can find the coefficient of friction directly by using a computer hooked up to force probes. To do this, divide the force needed to pull an object across a horizontal surface by the force of gravity acting on the object as it hangs on the force probe. You can probably borrow the probes from your school. Ask a physics teacher to show you how to use them.

Doing More
- Experiment with different shoe treads on different surfaces. Are some shoes better than others? Is one kind of tread good for all situations? Try to design the next top-selling sports shoe. Similarly, examine how different tire treads behave on different surfaces. Try to predict which treads will work better. You can get tread samples from a tire store, or use an old bicycle

How do car tires behave in ice?
Do they act the same way on sand?

tire. The store may even be able to supply worn tire treads. This will make your tests more realistic. How would you make a better tire tread?

- Examine how different size grains of sand affect the way objects slide down a ramp made of ice. How does the temperature of the ice change your results? Measure the average grain size with calipers or a micrometer. Is there a correlation between the size of the grains and the amount of sliding?

- Pull various objects through the water and investigate how friction is affected by an object's shape. Does the speed at which you pull have an effect on friction? Use a spring scale or force probes to obtain *quantitative* results—ones with specific values in *newtons* of force.

- Let a rough block of wood slide down a wooden ramp; and measure the coefficient of friction. Do this several times, sanding down the sliding surface of the block a little each time. Does the coefficient of friction change as the block becomes smoother? Keep performing the experiment until the surface of the block is very smooth. You can do a similar experiment by gradually sanding the surface of the ramp instead of the block.

MEASURING ACCELERATION IN THE REAL WORLD

You probably experience acceleration just about every day. Every time a car, a school bus, a train, or an airplane speeds up, the passengers accelerate too. Have you ever wondered why amusement park rides that involve acceleration are so thrilling? The following project will help you learn more about acceleration.

MAKING YOUR OWN ACCELEROMETER

What You Need	
Plastic protractor	Weight
Cardboard	Spring that stretches 1 to 2 cm when a large washer is on it
Pencil	
Scissors	Metal washer 2 to 3 cm in diameter
Tape	
String	Meterstick

You can build some simple devices to measure acceleration. You can then use these accelerometers to investigate how various accelerations make you feel.

To build your first accelerometer—Accelerometer A—place the protractor on the cardboard and trace around its edges with the pencil. Be sure to trace the hole on the protractor's flat edge, too. Remove the protractor from the cardboard. Copy the angles shown on the protractor onto the cardboard. See Figure 2. Next add the acceleration scale to the tracing of the protractor.

Now punch out the tracing of the protractor's hole and tie the string through it. Hang a weight from the other end of the string. The weight should be free to swing and be about 1 or 2 cm longer than the radius of the protractor.

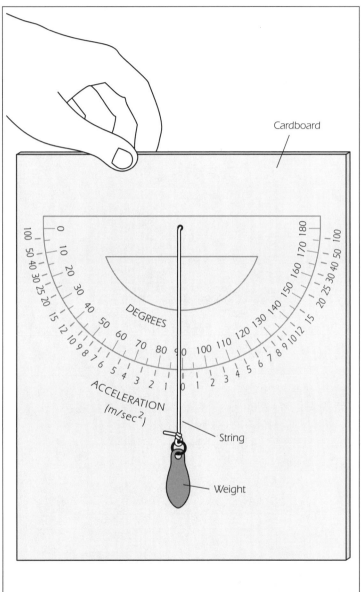

FIGURE 2 You can use this accelerometer to study accelerations along a horizontal plane.

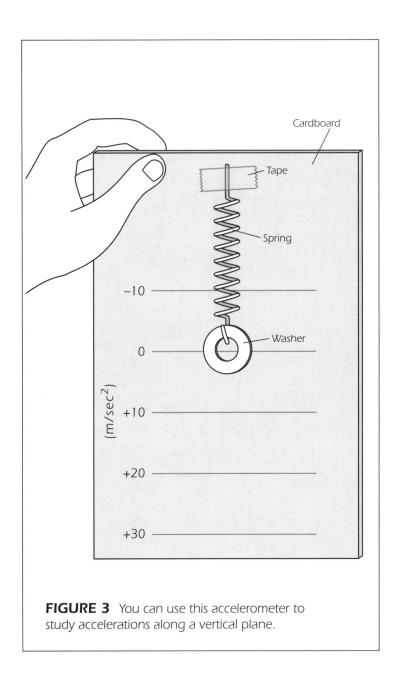

FIGURE 3 You can use this accelerometer to study accelerations along a vertical plane.

To make Accelerometer B, tape the spring to a $10 \times$ 15-cm piece of cardboard. Wherever the bottom of the spring falls, write "−10" on the cardboard. Attach the washer to the end of the spring with tape. Label the spot where the washer falls "0." Measure the distance between the −10 mark and the 0 mark. Write the numbers +10, +20, and +30 on the cardboard at intervals equal to the distance between the −10 and 0 marks. See Figure 3.

Your accelerometers measure units of acceleration in m/sec^2. An acceleration of 10 m/sec^2 means that *velocity* changes 10 meters per second every second. If an object's velocity changes 10 meters per second for 0.1 second, the object's total change in velocity would be 1 meter per second. If an object's velocity is constant or you are stationary, the acceleration is zero.

To use Accelerometer A, hold the piece of cardboard in front of you with the scale facing to the right or left. See Figure 4 on the next page. When you are stationary, the accelerometer should read zero. Now walk at a constant velocity in a straight line. Does the reading on the accelerometer change? Why or why not?

Starting from rest, move your body so the accelerometer reads 1 m/sec^2. How long can you keep this up? Record your observations in your notebook.

Velocity has direction, so when you change your direction, you change your velocity. This change in velocity results in an acceleration. *Centripetal acceleration* occurs when you move in a circle.

To experience centripetal acceleration, use tape to mark a circle 1 m in radius on the floor or ground. Hold the accelerometer in front of you with the scale facing you and walk around the circle at a speed that causes an acceleration of 1 m/sec^2. Record your observations.

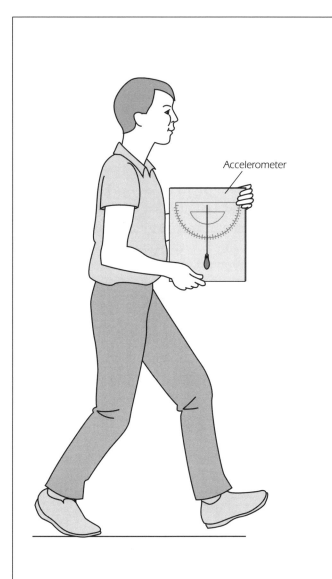

FIGURE 4 To use Accelerometer A, hold the piece of cardboard in front of you with the scale facing to the right or left as you walk forward.

Repeat the experiment at a centripetal acceleration of 2 m/sec^2 or 3 m/sec^2. You may find it easier to tie a string to a pole and walk around the pole with the string pulled taut to make sure you maintain a perfect circle—it's hard to watch your accelerometer and the circle on the floor at the same time.

The accelerations you have experienced so far have been in the horizontal plane (side-to-side). Now, use Accelerometer B to investigate vertical (up-and-down) accelerations. Hold Accelerometer B near the floor and then raise it with a constant 1 m/sec^2 acceleration. Try to move smoothly so that you will get a constant reading. Record your observations in your notebook. Repeat the procedure at several different accelerations.

Some companies, such as Vernier Software, sell accelerometers and force gauges that hook up to calculators. This kind of setup will give you very accurate acceleration readings. Repeat the experiment with the calculator set up. Are your results similar to the ones you obtained with your homemade accelerometer?

Doing More

- Use your accelerometer in a car. What accelerations occur as the car starts and stops, turns, and goes over bumps? Make notes of the sensations associated with these accelerations.

- Take Accelerometer A and Accelerometer B to an amusement park, and measure the accelerations you experience on a roller coaster. You may have to ride the roller coaster a couple of times to get accurate readings for each accelerometer. Record the values for various parts of the ride along with the sensations you feel. If you want some help understanding your

How do your accelerometers behave
as you ride a rollercoaster.

results, read *Amusement Park Physics* by Carole Escobar. A science fair project on this topic is sure to get the attention of other students and the judges.

- Build an accelerometer that uses a spring with a pencil or another object that can make a mark at the end. This will allow you to find values for acceleration in collisions that you can't experience. You may be able to devise an instrument that measures the acceleration of a ball that has just been hit by a bat. This is a very good place to use a computer accelerometer connected to a calculator.

ALTERING ACCELERATION

A collision occurs when two moving objects come into contact with each other. The result is a change in both objects' directions and/or velocities. The first kind of collision that probably comes to mind is a car accident, but there are many other kinds of collisions. For example, a baseball player can hit a home run when the bat comes into contact with a baseball.

We would like to make "bad" collisions less harmful and "good" collisions more powerful. That is why many cars have air bags and metal baseball bats were invented. How did the people who make cars and baseball bats think of these improvements? The answer has a lot to do with physics.

Before scientists could develop a better bat, they had to ask a few questions. What conditions allow a person to hitting a home run easier? How could a bat be designed to make it easier to hit a home run? Next, the researchers ran some tests. You can run your own test by doing the following procedure.

This girl has just forced the bat in her hands
to collide with the baseball.

THE FORCE OF A BASEBALL BAT

What You Need	
Baseball bat	Various kinds of balls
Rope	Meterstick
Support stand	Tape
Tabletop	Weights

Tie the rope to the handle of the baseball bat and hang it from the support stand. If you do this experiment outside, you can hang the bat from a tree branch. See Figure 5 on the next page. Otherwise, hang it from a nail driven into the wood molding of a doorway. *Caution: Ask an adult for permission before driving a nail into the doorway.* Place the table below the bat. Adjust the length of the rope so the bat will hit a ball placed at the edge of the table.

Place one of the balls on the edge of the table and mark the spot with a piece of tape. Pull the bat back several inches and mark the spot directly below it with another piece of tape. Now release the bat. It should swing smoothly and make contact with the ball.

Mark the spot where the ball lands with a third piece of tape. Using the meterstick, measure the distance from a point on the ground directly under the ball's initial position to where it lands. Repeat the experiment a couple of times, making the ball move in approximately the same direction after the collision. Record each distance and then calculate the average distance the ball traveled. Repeat this procedure for the other balls.

Do you think your results would be different if the bat were moving faster? Try pulling the bat back farther

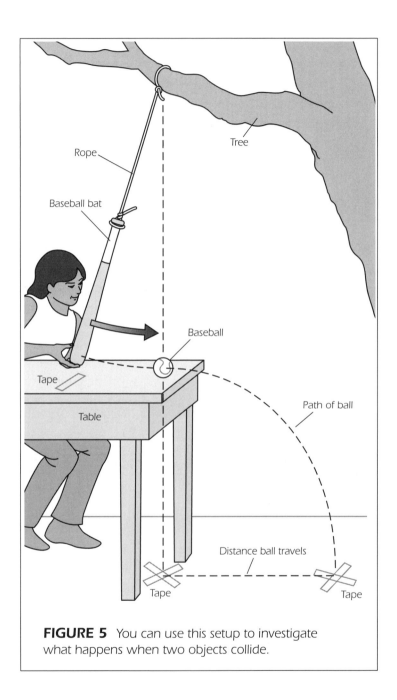

Rope

Tree

Baseball bat

Baseball

Tape

Path of ball

Table

Distance ball travels

Tape

Tape

FIGURE 5 You can use this setup to investigate
what happens when two objects collide.

during each trial to see what happens. Be sure to mark the new position of the bat with a piece of tape. Record each distance and then calculate the average distance each of the balls traveled. Did the balls behave as you expected?

Try to predict how far the first ball will go if you pull the bat back ever farther. It will be easier to make a good prediction if you put your data into a spreadsheet and graph it as you work. Look at the shape of the graph. With Vernier's *Graphical Analysis*, you can try different families of equations until you get one with a smooth curve. Repeat the procedure to test your prediction. Do the same for each of the other balls. How do the size, mass, and material of the ball affect your results?

As you learned earlier, when two objects collide, each one exerts a force on the other object and both change their motion. When a bat collides with a ball, the motion of both objects is affected. Repeat the procedure described above, but this time measure how the bat moves. After you have done a few trials, try to predict how the bat will move before you test each ball. Are your hypotheses accurate? What factors affect how the bat moves after the collision?

You may want to determine the actual velocities of the bat and ball. The velocity that the ball moves after the collision is related to the distance it travels horizontally before it hits the floor. If it travels twice as far, it is going twice as fast. You can calculate a ball's velocity, v, by dividing the horizontal distance, d, it travels by the time, t, it takes to fall to the floor (assuming it starts moving horizontally).

$$v = \frac{d}{t}$$

To calculate time, use the equation $t = \sqrt{h/4.9}$ where t is the time in seconds and h is the height in meters from which the ball falls or, in this case, the height of the table.

Before the bat swings, it has a lot of *potential energy*. As it moves, that potential energy is converted into *kinetic energy*. Potential energy is equal to *mgh* (mass × gravity × height). Kinetic energy is equal to $\frac{1}{2} mv^2$ [0.5 × mass (velocity × velocity)]. Since potential energy equals kinetic energy,

$$mgh = \frac{1}{2} mv^2$$
$$gh = \frac{1}{2} v^2$$
$$2gh = v^2$$
$$\sqrt{2gh} = v$$

In this case, g = 9.8 m/sec², so the velocity of the bat can be approximated by the equation $v = \sqrt{19.6h}$ where v is in m/sec and h is the difference in height in meters between where the tip of the bat is released and where it ends up. If you drop the bat from height h, it will fall with the velocity you calculated.

Try changing the mass of the bat by taping weights to it. How might this affect your results? Make a hypothesis and then test it. Do your results change depending on where you add the weights?

Doing More

- Repeat the procedure using a bat made from a different material. How do your results differ?

- Try to make a bat that will hit a ball the farthest with a given amount of swing. Test your bat. Do you think it would be good in a game? Would it work at the speeds baseball and softball pitchers normally throw balls?

- Devise a bat and ball that cannot be propelled very far. Would the materials you chose be good for protecting people if a car accident occurred?

- A collision is considered an *elastic collision* if kinetic energy is conserved and an *inelastic collision* if kinetic energy is lost. Lost kinetic energy generally does *work* on the objects that collide. If you are in an inelastic collision, work is done on your body. This work may break a bone.

   To find out whether kinetic energy is lost in a particular collision, compare the initial and final kinetic energy of the two objects. You can use the equation $K.E. = \frac{1}{2} mv^2$, where m is mass in kilograms and v is velocity in m/sec. Which collisions lose the most energy? the least?

- Design an apparatus in which both objects move before they collide. For example, you could tie rope to both objects and have them swing toward one another. Try connecting your objects with two ropes so you can make sure they always move in the same plane.

   You could use photoelectric "timing gates" hooked up to your computer to get accurate speeds of impact and rebounds. What happens to the energy in these collisions? Try modeling the collision of a boxing glove with a boxer's body. What happens when the boxer is moving toward the glove? away from it?

- When a pool ball is hit by a cue ball, both balls may be rolling. How is this different from a collision with a nonrolling ball? Design an experiment to model this kind of collision.

- When a car collides with a brick wall, the front end of the car collapses and absorbs energy. Experiment to see how each object in a chain reaction moves after a collision. Energy must be transferred from the first object to the second object, from the second object to the third object, and so on.

Do the results of your experiment show why auto manufacturers no longer make rear-engine cars (with little mass in front of the driver)? Try reading about modern car design and the concept of "crumple zones." Modern cars are designed to collapse and slow down the passenger compartment over the longest time possible.

Design an experiment to see which is safer for the passengers: having a large mass in front or having a front designed to "accordion." Use your accelerometer and calculations of velocities or a computer accelerometer and timing gates. You may find the following equation useful:

$$F\Delta t = m\Delta v$$

According to this equation, impulse equals change in *momentum*. F is force, Δt is the time of impact in seconds, m is the mass in kilograms, and Δv is the change in velocity (from some speed to zero). The longer you can make Δt, the smaller the force on the passengers, F, will be.

HOW THINGS BOUNCE: THE COEFFICIENT OF RESTITUTION

Many games involve balls that bounce off a bat, the floor, the ground, rackets, or each other. The way a ball bounces determines how the game is played. Playing tennis with "dead" tennis balls, which bounce very little, makes the game different and, most people think, less enjoyable. On the other hand, if a baseball bounced as high as a live tennis ball does when it is dropped onto a hard surface,

Tennis players know how to use their rackets to hit
a tennis ball over the net.

every baseball park in the world would have to be made
larger!

When scientists want to describe the way a ball
bounces, they use the term "coefficient of restitution." If
a ball hits the ground moving at 10 m/sec and leaves it
moving at 7 m/sec, its coefficient of restitution is 0.7 (7/10
= 0.7). As a matter of fact, 0.7 is the typical coefficient of

restitution of a tennis ball. A superball has a coefficient of restitution of about 1. It's "super" because it leaves a hard surface going at nearly the same speed as when it hit the ground. If a superball is dropped on a hard surface, it keeps bouncing for a long time. At the other extreme is a squash ball, which hardly bounces at all. Using a super-ball in a squash court would be dangerous because the ball would zip around so much that it would be hard to avoid getting hit.

To investigate which kinds of balls bounce best and how changing the bouncing surface can affect the coefficient of restitution, try the following project. You may want to develop some hypotheses before you perform each experiment.

BOUNCING BALLS

What You Need	
Two tennis balls, one new and one dead	Hard surfaces on which to drop the balls
Golf ball	Notebook paper
Rubber ball	Pencil
Styrofoam ball	Heavy weight
Meterstick	

Drop the golf ball on a hard surface from a height of 1 m. Measure the height to which the ball bounces. Record this value, and then drop the ball a few more times to see whether your results are consistent. Repeat the procedure with the rubber and Styrofoam balls.

Calculate the average height to which each ball rose, and use that value to determine the ball's coefficient of restitution, *CR*.

$$CR = \sqrt{h}$$

This equation works because the initial height is 1 m. If you were using a different initial height, you would have to use the equation $CR = \sqrt{h_{up}/h_{down}}$, where h_{up} is the height to which the ball bounces and h_{down} is the distance it falls.

Different balls have different coefficients of restitution because the balls were made in different ways or have changed since they were made. How do the coefficients of restitution differ between the golf, rubber, and Styrofoam balls? What might cause the differences?

Place the new tennis ball on a piece of paper, and trace the shape of the part touching the paper. Then place a heavy weight, such as a large stone, a log, or a bucket of water, on top of the ball. Trace the shape of the part of the ball touching the paper now. Remove the weight and the tennis ball from the paper, and write "new ball" next to the tracings. Place the dead tennis ball on the piece of paper, and repeat the procedure.

What differences do you notice in the tracings? Do the tracings help explain how the balls bounce? When a ball bounces, molecules in the ball rub against one another and energy is lost. The more the molecules rub, the more energy they lose. Does this explain why the balls bounce differently?

Try tracing the shape of the golf, rubber, and Styrofoam balls with no weight on them and then with weight on them. What do you find? Where is the "elastic" part of each ball? Can gas molecules rub against one another?

Now examine how various balls bounce on different surfaces. Drop the new tennis ball on a variety of surfaces, such as a concrete floor, a wood floor, carpets, clay, and grass. Find the ball's coefficient of restitution on each surface. How does a change in surface affect the coefficient of restitution of the other balls?

Doing More

- You can add air to kickballs, basketballs, soccer balls, and some brands of tennis balls to change the air pressure inside them. Develop a hypothesis for how air pressure affects the coefficient of restitution and then test it by adding air to a variety of balls. *Caution: If you add too much air to a ball, it may burst.* Take careful measurements, put them in a spreadsheet, and graph them.

- Suppose you wanted to design a new form of tennis that is played on a court half the size of a regular court. Taking into account that players must be able to hit the ball with a racket on this smaller court, figure out what coefficient of restitution you would like your ball to have. Test your hypothesis with some friends.

- When you drop a ball, it normally bounces several times before it comes to rest. Is a ball's coefficient of restitution related to the number of times it bounces? Design an experiment to find out. Because counting the last, small bounces may be difficult, you may want to set some limits on the size of the bounce. For example, if you drop the ball from 1 m, you might count all bounces more than 0.01 m high.

  You could also use a tape recorder or a camcorder to count the bounces. When you play the recording back at a slower speed, counting the number of bounces will be easier. You could even use a sound probe hooked up to a computer. It will give you a graphic record of the bounces. A software program, such as *Data Logger*, can count the bounces for you and automatically enter the numbers into a spreadsheet.

CHANGES IN ROTATIONAL MOTION

Some things are meant to turn, while others aren't. When you push on bicycle pedals, you expect the wheels of the bicycle to turn. You expect a screw to turn as it enters a piece of wood, but once the screw is in place, you expect it to stay there. When you use a tennis racket to hit a tennis ball, you expect the racket to keep moving in the same direction and not twist. If it twists, you may hit the ball in the wrong direction.

Why do some objects turn more easily than others? Before you can answer that question, you need to review some information you learned earlier. As you now know, when a force is exerted on a mass without an opposing force to balance it, acceleration occurs.

When you drive away from a stop sign while in a car (which has mass), the engine exerts an unbalanced force forward to accelerate the car. When you brake to a stop, an unbalanced force from the brakes causes a negative acceleration. When a car moves at a constant velocity, the forward force from the engine balances the backward force of friction.

When an object is moving in a straight line, acceleration is related to the force and the mass. When an object starts to rotate or changes its rate of rotation, it changes its *angular velocity*. The object's *angular acceleration* is caused by a *torque*—a force exerted at some distance from an axis of rotation. The angular acceleration is related to the torque and the *moment of inertia*. Moment of inertia is related to the object's mass and how far away it is from the axis of rotation.

Here's an example. It is easy to flip over a long wooden plank along its long axis. This is because all of the plank's mass is fairly close to its long axis. It is more difficult to turn the wooden plank along its short axis. See Figure 6. When the plank rotates around its long axis, the moment of inertia is small and the torque required to complete the task is small. When the plank rotates around

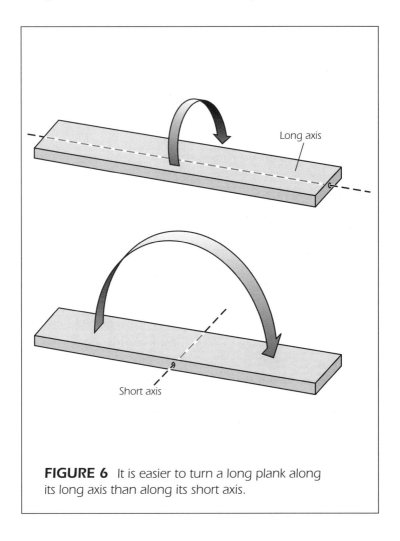

FIGURE 6 It is easier to turn a long plank along its long axis than along its short axis.

its short axis, the moment of inertia is larger and the torque required is larger too.

The experiments that follow will help you understand what torques are and how angular acceleration occurs.

A LOOK AT TORQUE

Place the pencil on a table or other flat surface and then place the center of the ruler on top of the pencil. See Figure 7. Roll the modeling clay into a cylinder of uniform thickness and then break it into four pieces of equal

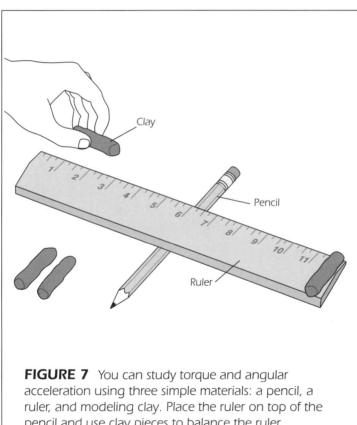

Clay

Pencil

Ruler

FIGURE 7 You can study torque and angular acceleration using three simple materials: a pencil, a ruler, and modeling clay. Place the ruler on top of the pencil and use clay pieces to balance the ruler.

What You Need	
Pencil	Ruler
Tabletop	Modeling clay

length. Each piece should have approximately the same mass. Place one piece of clay at one end of the ruler. Predict where you must place a second piece to balance the ruler. If you want to balance the ruler with three pieces of clay, where should each piece be placed? If you want to balance the ruler with four pieces of clay, where should each piece be placed? Test your hypothesis.

Torque is equal to force × distance from the axis of rotation. In this case, the pencil is the axis of rotation. If the torques are balanced, the ruler will be balanced. Is this true for your ruler and clay experiment? To find out, measure force in "units of clay." Measure all distances from the center of the ruler.

If you use a software program, such as *Graphical Analysis*, you can easily graph your data. Use the "curve fit" part of the software program to see what type of equation works best for your data.

TORQUE OF BICYCLE WHEELS

Turn the bicycle upside down, and tie a string about 20 cm (8 in.) long to a spoke on the front wheel. Tie a loop in the other end of the string and attach the spring scale. When you pull on the spring scale, the wheel should turn. See Figure 8. The force is exerted at a right angle to the spoke, so the force provides a torque that causes angular acceleration. Make a mark on the wheel with chalk so you can see when the wheel makes a complete revolution.

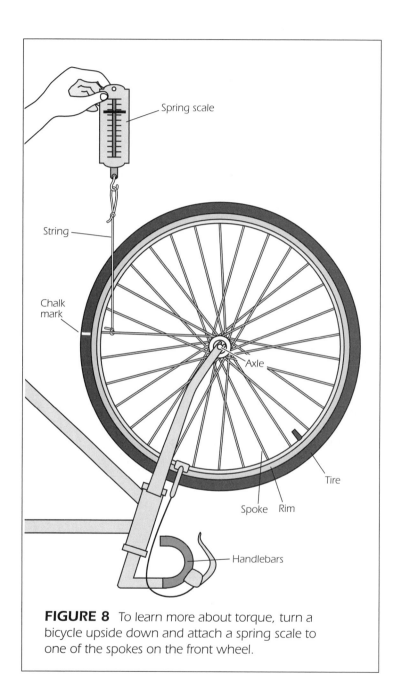

FIGURE 8 To learn more about torque, turn a bicycle upside down and attach a spring scale to one of the spokes on the front wheel.

Bicycle	Stopwatch
String	Tape
Spring scale	Metal bolts, 3 in. long and $\frac{1}{4}$ in. in diameter
Chalk	

With the wheel initially at rest, pull on the spring scale to exert a constant force on the wheel for 2 seconds. As soon as you exert the force, remove the spring scale from the string so the wheel is free to turn. (You may have to practice this step a few times.) Measure the time it takes the wheel to make two complete revolutions. Record the force exerted and the time required for two revolutions in a data table in your notebook or on a spreadsheet. Repeat the experiment with the same force until you get consistent results. Then find the average velocity by dividing the number of revolutions by the time.

Predict what will happen when you exert twice as much force or half as much force for the same period of time. Test your hypothesis. What happens to the angular velocity?

Move the spring scale so it is halfway between the rim and the hub of the wheel. How do the torque (force × radius) and angular acceleration change?* Be sure to record your results.

---

* Angular acceleration causes the wheel to change its angular velocity. Twice the torque should cause twice the angular acceleration and, in a given time, cause twice the change in velocity.

Move the string to other positions along the rim. How does each new position affect the way the wheel turns? Make sure that you exert the same force for the same amount of time. Record your results. What happens when you pull on the string in a direction parallel to the spokes?

Record your results, and then use all the data you have collected to create graphs. A computer program, such as *Graphical Analysis*, allows you to develop equations to fit the curve on a graph. Does your data fit a curve of linear, exponential, or trigonometric equations? You may want to ask a math teacher for help.

Using tape, attach the metal bolts around the rim of the wheel. Make sure the bolts are evenly spaced. Otherwise, the wheel will not spin evenly. The bolts increase the wheel's moment of inertia. As in the previous experiment, exert a torque on the wheel and determine the angular acceleration.

Move the weights closer to the wheel's axis and repeat the experiment. How do you think this will affect your results? Try the experiment to see if your hypothesis was correct.

Doing More

- When you hit a tennis ball, you don't want the racket to turn because the ball will go in an unpredictable direction. Using what you have discovered about torques and rotational motion, design a tennis racket that will not turn. Test your racket to see if it works better than a regular racket.

- As a screw enters a piece of wood, the torque from the screwdriver is greater than the torque from friction between the screw and the wood. After the screw is in the wood, frictional torque holds the screw in place.

Design an apparatus to find the torque needed to put a screw into wood. How does torque vary for different types of screws? Try screwing each kind of screw into a variety of materials. Can you predict which screws will work best in each material? Test your hypothesis, and then try to modify the screws so they will hold better or go into materials more easily.

- When you exert a force on the pedals of a bicycle, it is transferred to the rear wheel. The rear wheel then exerts a force on the ground to accelerate the bicycle.

You have to exert a torque to ride a bicycle.

How does acceleration change when the bicycle is in different gears? Use a spring scale or a force gauge on a computer to get quantitative results. Can you relate your results to the number of teeth on each gear?

- Imagine a tree blowing in the wind. If you think of the roots and ground as an axis, you will realize that the wind exerts a torque on the tree. Make models of trees of different heights and sizes to see how fast the wind must blow to knock them over. How strong does the trunk of the tree have to be to prevent snapping? Is the torque related to the height of the tree, the area of the leaves, or both?

- Investigate the torques exerted on a sailboat when the wind blows. What is required to keep the sailboat

What does torque have to do with sailing a boat?

upright? Use the Internet or the library to locate the design plans for a number of different sailboats. Record mast height, sail area, keel area, keel depth, keel mass, width, and length of each boat. Graph these data and look for patterns. Can you use *Graphical Analysis* to come up with equations for your data?

RIDING A BIKE WITH "NO-HANDS"

When you ride a bike "no-hands," if you lean to the right, the front wheel of the bike turns to the right. Your leaning is a rotation along an axis parallel to the direction in which you are traveling. The wheel turns, or *precesses*, around a vertical axis and turns to the right. If it weren't for precession, you wouldn't be able to ride a bike with "no-hands."

When you ride a bike, both wheels normally spin with the axis pointed horizontally. As a result, there is angular momentum around the horizontal axis perpendicular to the direction of motion. Angular momentum is determined by the mass of an object, how far the object is from the axis of rotation, and how fast and in what direction the object is spinning. If you lean to the right as you ride with "no-hands," the angular momentum of the wheel should change, too. But a rotating object, such as a bicycle wheel, always tries to conserve its angular momentum. Since your bicycle wheel tries to keep its original angular momentum, the wheel precesses and you turn.

Some bikes seem to be easier to ride "no-hands" than others. Did the designers of these bikes take precession into account when they built the bicycles? Is it possible to make a bicycle that can't be ridden "no-hands"? To find out more, try the following experiment.

BICYCLE WHEEL LEVITATION

What You Need	
Bicycle	Chalk
Rope that can support a bicycle wheel	Stopwatch
	Weights
A stand to hold the wheel	String

Take the front wheel off the bicycle and tie the rope to the axle, as shown in Figure 9 on the next page. Make sure the rope will not slip off. Use the chalk to mark the wheel so you can see when the wheel makes a complete revolution.

Exert a force on the wheel so that it starts spinning. At this point, the axle should be pointed horizontally. If the wheel is spinning fast enough, it will not fall immediately. The motion you observe is precession. Record your observations.

Spin the wheel again and count how many revolutions it makes in 10 seconds. Next, time how long it takes for the bicycle wheel to precess, or spin on another axis, one complete revolution. Record all your data in a table in your notebook or in a spreadsheet.

In the experiments described above, the gravitational force on the wheel has provided the torque that causes precession. Tie weights to a string attached to the side of the wheel opposite from where the rope supports the wheel. What happens to the rate of precession?

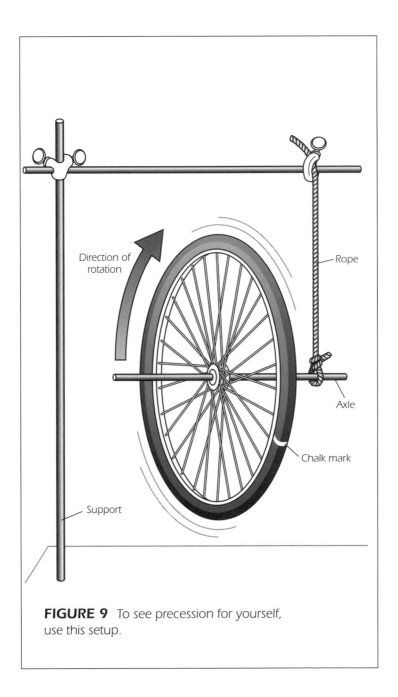

Direction of rotation

Rope

Axle

Chalk mark

Support

FIGURE 9 To see precession for yourself, use this setup.

What happens when you spin the wheel in the opposite direction?

What do you think will happen to the rate of precession if the mass of the wheel is changed? To test your hypothesis, tape weights along the rim. The weights should be evenly spaced so the wheel will spin smoothly.

Doing More

- How does a Frisbee's tilt affect the direction in which it flies? Try placing some weights along the rim of the Frisbee. How should the weights be placed to keep

How does a Frisbee's tilt affect
the direction in which it flies?

the Frisbee going straight? Try throwing a Frisbee with your left hand, and then with your right hand. What happens when you spin the Frisbee in opposite directions?

- Make a model of a hard disk drive for a computer and examine the forces acting on the axle of the drive when the computer is bumped, forcing the "wheel" to tip. Does the disk's diameter affect the results?

- Experiment with the rate of rotation of a football. How does it change the direction in which the ball points during flight?

- Design and build a rotating wheel that will fit inside a suitcase. Ask a friend or parent to watch you as you walk with the suitcase. The precession of the wheel in the suitcase will cause the suitcase to behave very strangely. You may want to use an electric motor to keep the wheel spinning.

TEMPERATURE AND PRESSURE

Molecules are always in motion. They move faster when they are warm and slower when they are cold. At low temperatures, materials usually exist as solids. At high temperatures, materials usually exist as gases. In between, materials usually exist as liquids. Pressure also influences whether a material exists as a solid, a liquid, or a gas.

EXPANSION AND CONTRACTION

The molecules in a solid are generally packed more tightly than the molecules in a liquid, and the molecules in a liquid are packed more tightly than the molecules in a gas. In most cases, when a material is heated, it expands.

The engineer who designed this bridge made the expansion joint look like a decorative element.

As a result, the same number of molecules occupy a larger space. When a material is cooled, it usually contracts.*

In some cases, the expansion and contraction of materials can cause problems. For example, if the materials in a building or bridge expand at different rates on a hot day,

---

* The notable exception to this rule is water. Water at 4°C expands when it warms up *and* when it cools down. Ice has a greater volume than liquid water because the molecules form crystals. If ice is cooled further, it will contract.

the structure may fall apart. This is why engineers design many bridges with special expansion joints. However, if materials did not expand or contract when the temperature changes, thermometers and thermostats would not work.

How much do materials expand or contract when their temperature changes? Do different materials expand or contract different amounts under the same conditions? By experimenting to find the answers to these questions, you can begin to understand the problems some architects, engineers, and scientists face every day.

THE EXPANSION OF WATER

What You Need	
500-mL round bottomed flask	Two-holed stopper
Cold water	30-cm piece of glass tubing
Glycerin	Ruler
Thermometer	

Fill the flask with water. Lubricate the thermometer with glycerin and carefully insert it into one hole in the stopper.* Lubricate the glass tubing with glycerin and carefully insert it into the other hole in the stopper. *Caution: Be careful when working with glass. If the thermometer or glass tubing breaks, clean it up immediately and try not to cut yourself.*

---

* Instead of the thermometer, you could use a temperature probe connected to a computer or calculator. If you choose this setup, use a one-holed stopper.

Insert the stopper into the flask, as shown in Figure 10 on the next page. The water level inside the glass tubing should be about 2.5 cm above the top of the stopper. Measure the exact distance and record it in your notebook or on a spreadsheet. Take a temperature reading every minute for several minutes. When the temperature is constant, record the value.

Hold the flask in your hands until the temperature rises 5°C. Record the new temperature and the distance the water has risen. Repeat this procedure until the temperature stops rising. Create a graph of your data. What does the graph tell you about the expansion of water?

Disassemble your equipment as soon as you are done with this procedure. If you don't, the glycerin may cause the glassware to stick to the stopper.

Doing More

- Repeat the experiment using ice chips instead of cold water. *Caution: Do not place a flask filled with water in a freezer. When the water expands, the flask may break.* Are your results any different?

- Predict what will happen when you place the apparatus in a pan of boiling water. *Caution: Do not hold the flask over a direct heat source and be careful not to burn yourself.* Do your results match your hypothesis? Find the coefficient of expansion, β, by dividing the change in volume of the liquid (the cross-sectional area of the tube times the distance the water moves), ΔV, by the total volume of the liquid, V, times the change in temperature, ΔT.

$$\beta = \frac{\Delta V}{(V \times \Delta T)}$$

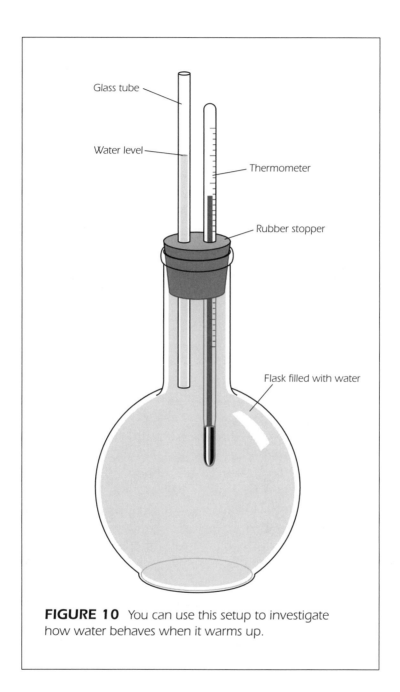

Glass tube

Water level

Thermometer

Rubber stopper

Flask filled with water

FIGURE 10 You can use this setup to investigate how water behaves when it warms up.

MEASURING EXPANSION AND CONTRACTION

What You Need	
0.5- to 1-m piece of rubber tubing	Protractor
0.5- to 1-m piece of metal tubing	Pencil
	T-pin
Funnel	Tape
Ring stand with iron ring	Tabletop
	Large bucket
2.5-cm piece of rubber tubing	Ice bucket
Scissors	Ice water
	Hot water
Cardboard	Thermos

Attach the 0.5- to 1-m piece of rubber tubing to the metal tubing. Attach the other end of the rubber tubing to the neck of the funnel. Place the funnel in the ring stand.

Place the 2.5-cm piece of rubber tubing near the other end of the metal tubing. Using the scissors, cut a 20-cm disk out of cardboard. Using the protractor and a pencil, mark off every 10 degrees on the edge of the cardboard disk. To create a dial, push the T-pin through the center of the disk and tape it in place. Place the apparatus near the edge of the table with the needle of the dial under the short length of rubber tubing, as shown in Figure 11. The edge of the metal tubing should extend over the edge of the table. Place the large bucket on the floor so it will catch water that flows through the apparatus.

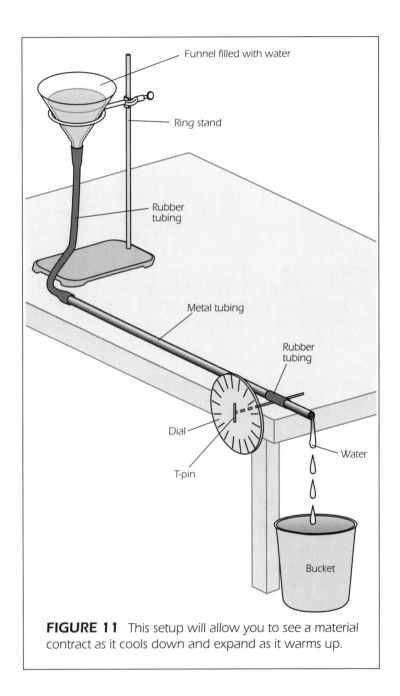

FIGURE 11 This setup will allow you to see a material contract as it cools down and expand as it warms up.

Notice the position of the dial and then pour ice water from the ice bucket into the funnel so it flows through the tubing. As the tubing cools down, it should contract and the dial should turn. Record the direction and amount the disk turns.

Predict what will happen when you pour hot water from the thermos through the tubing. Do your results match your hypothesis?

Doing More

- Repeat the procedure, but this time, record the temperature of the ice water and hot water before pouring it through the apparatus. Create a graph of the water temperatures versus the amount of expansion. Also, try using a few different types of tubing—copper, aluminum, glass, and steel. Do you observe any differences in your results? Calculate the coefficient of linear expansion, α, which is the amount of expansion, ΔL, divided by the length of the tube, L, and the temperature change, Δt.

$$\alpha = \frac{\Delta L}{(L \times \Delta t)}$$

To find the amount of expansion, ΔL, multiply the circumference of the T-pin and the angular distance the disk turns.

- Using a flask of water (you might add food coloring) and a small glass tube, build a thermometer. Is your homemade thermometer as accurate as the ones you buy in a store? If you add antifreeze to your thermometer, you can measure temperatures below freezing. *Caution: Make sure you buy antifreeze made from propylene glycol. Antifreeze made from ethylene glycol is poisonous.*

TRACING THE FLOW OF HEAT

Heat always travels from warmer materials to cooler ones. Some materials, such as metals, are good conductors of heat; others, such as Styrofoam, are good insulators. In metals, molecules are generally fairly close together, so it is easy for heat to be transferred from molecule to molecule.

How long do you think the coffee
in this cup will stay warm?

Studying heat transfer has many practical applications. Scientists can find the best way to keep a house warm in the winter and cool in the summer. They can design a coffee mug that will keep coffee warm for hours and a thermos that will keep lemonade cool at a picnic. They can even learn how warm-blooded animals survive in deserts or polar regions and how cold-blooded creatures regulate their body temperature. The following project will introduce you to the concept of heat transfer.

KEEPING LIQUIDS HOT (OR COLD)

What You Need	
Cups made of Styrofoam, metal, glass, plastic, and paper	Thermometer
	Index cards that are wider than the opening of the cups
Measuring cup	
Hot water	Stopwatch

Fill one of the cups with hot water until it is half full. *Caution: Make sure that you don't get scalded by the water.* Record the amount of water you added to the cup in a data table in your notebook or in a spreadsheet.

Using the thermometer or a temperature probe hooked up to a computer, measure the temperature of the water. Record this value in your table too. Cover the cup with an index card. (Poke a hole in the card for the thermometer.)

After 2 minutes have passed, measure the temperature again. Continue recording the time and the temperature at 2-minute intervals until 10 minutes have passed. Set the cup aside for 10 more minutes and then take a final temperature.

Repeat this procedure using the other cups. For each cup, create a graph of the temperature (vertical axis) versus time (horizontal axis). Which material is the best conductor? Which is the best insulator? What happens to the rate of cooling as time goes by?

Repeat the procedure, but do not place a card over each cup. What effect does a lid have on each cup? Repeat the procedure using two or three Styrofoam cups—one inside another. What happens?

If you have access to several temperature probes, try to find out whether there are any slight differences in temperature within each the cup? Put probes at different depths in the cups and conduct the experiment again. If you do detect "microclimates," which part of the cup needs the most insulation to keep a liquid hot for long periods of time?

Are you surprised by your results? Does the density of a material affect the rate at which heat flows through it? What do you think is happening at the molecular level?

Doing More

- Repeat the procedure using a large container, such as a picnic cooler or a large pot, instead of the cups. Does the experiment work with larger quantities of water and larger surface areas? You may have to take the temperature at longer time intervals to see changes.

- All objects in a room are at the same temperature, but some of them feel cooler than others. Does the experiment described above help you explain the differences you feel?

Try setting out three bowls of water: one containing fairly hot tap water, one with room temperature water, and one with very cold water. Put one hand in the hot water and one in the cold water. After 30 seconds, place both hands in the room temperature bowl. Do your hands feel the same water temperature? Are your hands actually feeling temperature or heat flow?

- Design an experiment to find out what happens when fiberglass housing insulation is wet with differing amounts of water. What does your experiment tell you about the need to keep fiberglass insulation dry? What happens to the insulating properties of down or other materials used in sleeping bags when they are wet? Which materials seem to insulate best when wet?

- Design an experiment to find the temperature of a damp object when a fan blows air over it. Does the humidity of the air affect your results? You can find the humidity in your area by checking the weather bureau, a local television station, or *http://www.weather.com* on the Internet. Because humidity varies during the day, try to find a value that was recorded at the time you performed the experiment. Do the same experiment on a day when the humidity is different. Record your results in a spreadsheet and create a graph. Can you think of a way to use your experimental setup to determine what the humidity is at any time?

- Experiment with different building materials to find out whether they are good insulators. Which are best at keeping heat in? Which are best at keeping cool air in?

- Find two houses that are about the same size and use the same kind of fuel, such as oil or gas. Ask each owner how the home is insulated and how much fuel is required to heat it during the winter. How does the insulation affect heat loss? What other factors make a difference in the amount of heat lost by a house during the heating season?

Check with your local utility company or look on the Internet to get more information about energy usage and strategies for making homes energy efficient. It may be difficult to get good data for this project because there are so many variables. But don't get frustrated, you may learn a lot from what you can measure.

HOW TO TRAP THE SUN'S ENERGY

Solar energy is free, but it takes money to build devices that can collect it. Because finding inexpensive ways to collect this nonpolluting energy is important for the world, scientists are interested in learning what kinds of collectors are best for a given situation. Is it possible to design collectors simple and inexpensive enough for people in developing nations to build and operate? A few experiments with solar collectors can help you find out.

BUILDING A SOLAR COLLECTOR

Cut a piece of aluminum foil the same size as the bottom of the pan, and place it in the bottom of one baking pan. Cut a piece of black plastic the same size as the bottom of the pan, and place it in the bottom of the other pan. You may need to add a little bit of sand to keep the plastic on the bottom of the pan. Fill both baking pans with water of the same temperature.

Using the thermometer, record the initial water temperature in each pan and then place both pans in the sun. (You could use a temperature probe hooked up to a com-

What You Need	
Aluminum foil	Sand
Scissors	Water
Two identical baking pans	Thermometer
	A sunny day
Black plastic	Plastic wrap

puter instead of a thermometer.) When 5 minutes have passed, measure the water temperature again and record your results in a data table in your notebook or in a spreadsheet. When you make the graph, place time on the horizontal axis and temperature on the vertical axis. Continue to record the temperature of each pan every 5 minutes for at least an hour. Which pan seems to be a better solar collector?

Repeat your experiment, starting with water at the same temperature, but put plastic wrap over one of the pans. How does the plastic wrap affect your results? Continue measuring the temperature every 30 minutes for several hours. Does the rate of temperature change differ over time? Why or why not? Make sure that the conditions don't change and that you have the same amount of sun at about the same angle for all your trials.

Doing More
- Replace the aluminum foil and black plastic with other materials. You might try materials with different colors, such blue, green, or red. Do the new materials collect heat more or less efficiently? If one color seems

to absorb heat better, try different materials of that color. When using foil, does it make a difference whether the shiny side or dull side is up?

- Design a collector with reflectors that focus more sunlight on it. Does the water heat up twice as fast when you reflect light from twice the area?

- Examine what happens if air blows across the pan of water. You might need a fan to provide a constant stream of air for a controlled experiment. Try a three-speed fan and graph your results. Do differences in fan speed change the results?

- What happens when you cover the pan with more than one layer of plastic wrap? Does the angle at which the sun's rays hit the cover affect your results? Try using bubble wrap instead of plastic wrap. Is there a difference?

- Design a solar collection system with a pump that allows you to tilt the collector so that it is perpendicular to the sun. Design the system so that water flows across the collection surface. Does this system collect more heat? Is it worth the extra cost of a pump? You can buy a very small pump at a local nursery or garden center.

- By evaluating the efficiency of your collectors, you can find out whether it would be worthwhile to build a large-scale collector that works the same way. To do this, multiply the milliliters of water heated by the temperature change. The result is *calories*. One calorie equals 4.185 joules. Home heating and cooling companies often use British Thermal Units (BTUs),

The windows and solar panels on this home
collect energy from the sun's rays.

which equal 1,054.5 joules or 252 calories. This should help you make sense of BTU ratings on furnaces, air conditioners, and water heaters.

Can you make your collector large enough to provide all the heat and hot water a house needs? Would the collector be reliable? Would it be possible to collect energy all year long or just in the summer?

- Design a system for measuring the amount of heat absorbed by a collector in one day. Hint: Temperature probes with long leads to the computer may be very helpful here. Test the system on several different types of collectors. Which collector works best over the course of the day?

BERNOULLI'S PRINCIPLE

The *pressure* of a fluid—a gas or a liquid—changes depending on how quickly it is flowing. The faster a fluid travels, the lower its pressure. This physical law is known as Bernoulli's principle. It was named after Daniel Bernoulli, a Swiss scientist who lived in the late 1700s. Bernoulli's principle explains how airplanes fly, why water moves up a straw when you blow across the top of it, and why you can suspend a Ping-Pong ball in the stream of air from a vacuum cleaner's exhaust hose or a hair dryer. The next activity will help you find out more about Bernoulli's principle.

THE FORCE OF YOUR BREATH

Cut a strip of paper about 2.5 cm wide and 10 cm long, and hold it just above your mouth. Blow out through your mouth at a constant speed and observe the result. Now place the strip just below your mouth. What do you think will happen when you blow the strip of paper? Test your

What You Need	
Paper	Tape
Scissors	Stopwatch

hypothesis. Do you get different results if you blow with more or less force?

Blow over the paper at a constant speed until it is moving at a constant rate. Time how long it takes to empty your lungs of air. Record the time in your notebook. *Caution: Be careful that you don't hyperventilate. If you start to feel dizzy, take a break from your experiment. You can also use a three-speed fan with a large funnel in front of it to get a constant flow of air.*

Tape another 2.5 × 10 cm paper strip on top of the first piece. This will double the weight of the paper. Blow over the top of the paper at a constant speed until the paper is at a constant position. Did you have to blow harder than when you used only one piece of paper? Time how long it takes to empty your lungs. Compare that time to the one you recorded when you blew on just one strip of paper.

Doing More

• Connect a vacuum cleaner hose to its air outlet, which blows air out instead of sucking it in. Bend the hose so that the air stream flows past a flat object, such as a small piece of cardboard. Use a sensitive spring scale to measure the force. (You may need to borrow this from your school's science lab.) Vary the speed at which the air moves past the cardboard by moving the hose closer to, or farther from, the cardboard. How does the force vary with the angle, speed, and size of the cardboard?

- Examine the forces exerted on a Ping-Pong ball when it is placed in a stream of air from a hair dryer. Be sure to use the cool setting so the ball won't melt. What determines the force exerted on the ball? What happens if you use a ball with a different mass or size? Can you change the way the air leaves the hair dryer to get a better effect?

CHAPTER 5

PROPERTIES
OF
MATTER

All matter has properties that determine how it behaves under certain conditions. In this chapter you will look at three properties of matter—permeability, solubility, and buoyancy. *Permeability* is a property that describes how easily molecules migrate from one area to another. Materials composed of large molecules are more permeable than materials made up of small molecules.

You probably know that some materials dissolve in water, while others don't. *Solubility* is a property that describes how well one material dissolves in another.

When several materials are placed in a container, the denser ones sink to the bottom while the more buoyant ones rise to the top. In some materials, such as water, molecules on the surface pull together to create a durable outer layer. You will learn more about various properties of matter in this chapter.

A LOOK AT PERMEABILITY

Have you ever wondered why very few plants can grow on the beach, but thousands of different plants are found in a temperate or tropical rain forest? The answer to this

The plants of this forest are part of a complex ecosystem. The soil they grow in holds water long enough for their roots to absorb it.

question has a lot to do with the soil. A beach is covered with sand. When rain falls, water quickly drains down through the sand. Since sand cannot hold water, few plants grow in it.

The soil in a forest is very different. It contains some sand, but it also contains clay, silt, and all kinds of dead plant matter. Rainwater moves through these materials more slowly. Some of the water that stays in the upper layers of soil can be absorbed by plant roots.

Scientists say that sand is very permeable, while clay and silt are semipermeable. Liquids, such as water, pass through semipermeable materials much more slowly than through permeable material.

THE PERMEABILITY OF SAND

What You Need	
Two measuring cups Sand	Water

Add sand to one measuring cup until it is half full. Add water to the other measuring cup until it is half full. Pour the water into the sand a little at a time. After adding some water, wait until it sinks into the sand before adding more. Stop adding water when no more soaks into the sand. Measure the amount of water left in the measuring cup, and subtract that from the original amount of water to find out how much water soaked into the sand.

Do your results surprise you? Where did the water go? Repeat the experiment using differing amounts of sand and water. Enter your results in a spreadsheet and create a graph.

To find the actual volume of sand, use the following equation

$$d = \frac{m}{v}$$

where d stands for density, m stands for mass in grams, and v stands for volume in milliliters. You can find the density of sand by looking up silicon dioxide—the main ingredient in sand—in a density table. Ask a science teacher for assistance. How much of the "sand" sample was really air?

Doing More
- Repeat the experiment using different types of sand and gravel. Is there a difference in the amount of water you can add? Do different types of sand contain different amounts of air?

- Repeat the experiment using marbles instead of sand. Before you begin, try to predict how much water you will be able to add.

STUDYING SOLUBILITY
You probably know what happens if you add a teaspoon of sugar to coffee—it dissolves. Sugar is soluble in coffee. What do you think would happen if you added a teaspoon of rice to coffee? Nothing would happen because rice is insoluble in coffee.

Have you ever wondered why some materials dissolve and others do not? It has to do with attraction between particles in the two substances. To find out more about solubility, try the following project.

MAKING SUGAR AND SALT DISAPPEAR

What You Need	
Two measuring cups	Spoons
Warm water	Salt
Granulated sugar	

Add warm water to the first measuring cup until it is half full. Add sugar to the second measuring cup until it is half full. Add a little bit of the sugar to the warm water and stir the mixture until the sugar dissolves completely. Record the volume of sugar left in the measuring cup and the new volume of the sugar-water mixture.

Keep adding sugar to the water a little at a time. Each time you add sugar, record the amount of sugar left in the measuring cup and the volume of the sugar-water mixture. How much sugar will dissolve in the water? When no more sugar will dissolve, keep adding sugar. When you have added all the sugar, record the total volume of the sugar-water mixture.

How is this experiment different from the The Permeabilty of Sand experiment on pages 80 and 81? What happens to the volume of the sugar-water mixture when no more sugar will dissolve?

Repeat the same procedure with salt instead of sugar. A salt crystal is held together by ionic bonds, while a sugar crystal is held together by covalent bonds. Does this difference explain any differences between the procedure involving sugar and the procedure involving salt?

Doing More

- Add rubbing alcohol or salad oil to a measuring cup half full of water. How does the volume of the water change when a given volume of one of these substances is added?

- How does changing the temperature of water change the amount of sugar that will dissolve in it? What happens when the solution cools down? What happens if you throw a few sugar crystals into a solution that has cooled very slowly? Try the same experiment with a salt solution. Hint: You will have better results if you use canning salt or kosher salt.

A LOOK AT BUOYANCY

Some things float, and others sink. Have you ever wondered why? If the downward force exerted by gravity is greater than the upward force exerted by a fluid, an object will sink. This upward force is called *buoyancy*. The denser a fluid is, the more upward force it can exert. For example, corn syrup is more dense than water, so some things that sink in water will float in corn syrup. Most objects "sink" in air because it has a very low density.

Why do some people float in the water and others sink? Why is it easier to float in the ocean than in freshwater? Why does a boat sink farther into the water as it is loaded with cargo? Why do rocks feel lighter when you lift them in the water than when you lift them out of the water?

Think about these questions as you perform the following project. Knowing the equation for calculating water pressure will come in handy.

$$P = \rho g d$$

Believe it or not, some liquids are denser than some
solids. That is why a penny can float on mercury.

In this equation, P is the pressure in newtons/m^2, ρ is the density of the fluid in kg/m^3, g is the acceleration of gravity in m/sec^2 (about 10 on the surface of Earth), and d is the depth in meters.

MEASURING BUOYANCY

What You Need	
Metal, wood, and rubber objects	Pitcher with straight sides that holds at least 1.9 L of water
20-cm piece of strong, lightweight string	Pen
Spring scale	Wooden stick slightly shorter than the pitcher
Ruler	

Tie one object to a 20-cm piece of string. Attach the spring scale to the other end of the string. Determine the force exerted on the spring scale by the object and record the value in your notebook. Lower the object into the pitcher of water until it is covered with water or it starts to float. Now what is the force exerted on the spring scale? Record the value. (If the object floats, the force will be zero.)

Repeat the procedure with the other objects. Before you test each one, predict whether each will float. Were your hypotheses correct? Remember to record all your data in your notebook.

Use the pen to mark and label 10-cm increments on the wooden stick. Tie a 20-cm piece of string to the stick. Attach the other end of the string to the spring scale, and find the force exerted on the spring scale by the object.

Lower the stick into the pitcher and measure the force at each mark. Does the water exert twice as much pressure against the stick when it is lowered twice as far into the pitcher? Does this make sense according to the equation for water pressure?

Doing More

- Make a hydrometer, a device that measures the density of a liquid, by filling one end of a plastic soda straw with some sand. Clamp one end of the straw with a paper clip so the sand will stay in the straw. Drop the hydrometer in a container of water, and use a pen to draw how far it sinks. Now add sugar or salt to the water to change its density. Make a new mark to indicate how far the hydrometer sinks. Try this with other fluids. *Caution: Before using any fluid, check with an adult to make sure it is safe.*

  Calculate the density of each fluid using the equation

  $$\text{density} = \frac{\text{mass}}{\text{volume}}$$

  Now you can use the hydrometer to estimate the densities of additional fluids, such as water samples containing varying amounts of salt.

- Use a plastic soda bottle and a small rubber tube to build a model of a submarine. Put some sand in the bottle. Make two holes in the bottle cap, and stick the rubber tube in one of the holes. By blowing air in or sucking it out, you can make the bottle float or sink.

- Some people float and some sink. Some float when their lungs are full of air, but sink when they exhale. Can you explain why? What can a person do to increase the chances that he or she will float? If a person makes a bubble of air in his or her swimsuit, will he or she be more likely to float? Using the Internet or a library, find the density of water in the ocean, the Great Salt Lake in Utah, and the Dead Sea in the Middle East. Where would people float most easily?

WHAT IS SURFACE TENSION?

The molecules on the surface of a fluid pull on one another, and the molecules below them pull down on the top layer. As a result, the surface of a fluid is relatively strong. The *surface tension* of water is great enough that some small animals, such as fisher spiders and water

Surface tension makes it possible for a fisher spider to rest on the water's surface.

striders, can actually walk on water. In the next project, you will learn more about the surface tension of water.

THE STRENGTH OF WATER'S SURFACE

What You Need	
Baking pan	Spring scale that can measure thousandths of a newton
Water	
Fine wire	Liquid dishwashing soap
Dropper	

Add water to the baking dish until it is half full. Using the wire, make a small loop and attach it to the spring scale. Use the spring scale to find the weight of the wire when it is out of the water. Be sure to record this value in your notebook.

Next, lower the wire into the water and use the spring scale to find the force as you remove the wire from the water. Record the maximum value. The difference between the first reading and the second is the surface tension.

Change the shape and length of the wire and repeat the procedure. Do you get different results? Does the force double when the length of the wire in the water is doubled? Are any shapes of wire capable of increasing the surface tension? Use a program, such as *Graphical Analysis*, to graph your data and find an equation that fits your results.

Add the liquid dishwashing soap to the water one drop at a time, and observe the changes in the force required to remove the wire from the water. (Make sure all the wire exits the water at the same time.) Can you find a mathematical way to show the relationship between the number of drops of soap and the surface tension?

Doing More

- Surface tension makes the surface area of a liquid as small as possible. Observe how soap film attaches to wire loops of different shapes. Does it always choose the smallest surface area that still touches all the wire?

   Make a wire cube or tetrahedron. What happens to the film? Can you find a way to photograph this for a science fair presentation? Is there a way that people at the science fair can make films themselves? Audience participation gets the attention of judges.

- Place some drops of water on a piece of waxed paper. How is their shape related to their size? Use calipers or a micrometer to accurately measure their diameter and height. Do these drops magnify newsprint placed underneath the waxed paper? Judge how much bigger or smaller the images are. Is the amount of magnification related to the size of the drop?

- Look at several books that provide instructions for making soap bubbles. Can you develop a better mixture for making bubbles? Should you use a different mixture to make large bubbles and small bubbles? Can you figure out how to make bubbles that will last a long time? Remember to experiment with only one variable at a time.

CHAPTER 6

VIBRATIONS, ELECTRICITY, AND MAGNETISM

A vibration is a steady, repetitive motion. When a car goes over a bump, it bounces, or vibrates, until the car's shock absorbers stop the motion. When you hold one end of a plastic ruler against a table, exert a force on the other end, and then release it, the ruler vibrates up and down. When electricity flows as an *alternating current*, an electric field causes charged particles to vibrate back and forth.

In this chapter, you will first learn about vibrations. Then you will find out how vibrations are involved in the flow of electric current. You will also learn how and why power plants use magnetic fields to generate electricity.

A LOOK AT VIBRATIONS

When you pluck a guitar string, it vibrates and produces a sound. When wind blows at a constant speed, a tree sways to and fro at a particular *frequency*. A small tree has a different frequency than a large one.

When the strings of a guitar vibrate, we hear a sound. Depending on how this musician plays his guitar, that sound may be loud and harsh or soft and sweet.

An object's frequency is determined by its mass and the amount of force required to move the object back to its *equilibrium position*—the point at which the forces acting upon an object are balanced.

When you are not playing a guitar, its strings are straight and the forces acting upon it are balanced. When you pluck a string, it moves away from its equilibrium position. A counter force works to restore the string's equilibrium. If the string is tightened, it will exert more force when it is moved away from its equilibrium point. With a larger force, the string will accelerate more quickly and vibrate faster. You hear a different sound because the string's vibration frequency has changed.

On a much smaller scale, the vibration frequency of a water molecule in a microwave oven is related to the mass of the molecule and the force causing the molecule to accelerate. Because water molecules have a very small mass, they vibrate billions of times a second.

Do large objects always vibrate at lower frequencies than small objects? Is it always possible to predict an object's vibration frequency? The following project will help you answer these questions.

RUBBER BAND OSCILLATIONS

Stretch a rubber band between two solid supports, such as the legs of a table. Tape a pencil to the center of the rubber band. Pull the pencil down and release it. How long does it take for the pencil to move up and down ten times?* Record your results. You could use a photogate hooked up to a computer or a force gauge; these can automatically place your data in a spreadsheet. Repeat the

---

* If the pencil bounces up and down too fast to record the time, weigh the rubber band down with additional pencils or reduce the tension in the rubber band by moving the supports closer together.

What You Need	
Rubber bands	Tape
Two supports	Stopwatch
Pencils	

experiment and average your data. Use your average to determine the length of one cycle.

Add another pencil to the rubber band and repeat the experiment. How do your results differ? Try adding even more pencils. What happens? You could also modify the experiment by changing the tension on the rubber band or by using more than one rubber band.

Doing More

- Use a setup that includes springs to determine what factors affect the *period* of a vibrating object.

- Use clamps to attach a plastic ruler to a solid table. *Caution: Be careful not to damage the table.* About 3 cm of the ruler should be on the table; the rest should be in the air. Push down on the ruler so that it begins to bounce. Find the ruler's period of vibration.

  A diving board moves in the same way when a person jumps off it. How do you think designers plan for this kind of bouncing? Change the length of board hanging off the table. Does the board's vibration frequency change?

- Experiment with a pogo stick. Is it possible to change the rate at which the stick bounces up and down? Is the rate the same for all people who use the stick? What could you do to change the period of the pogo stick?

- Have you ever spun a coin on its edge? Right before it stops and falls over, you can hear a noise that sounds like "wha-wha-wha-wha-wha." What determines the frequency of this vibration? Can you predict the frequency before you test it? Do larger disks behave the same way?

- How fast do you think a bird beats its wings? If you have access to a video camera, try to film a bird in flight and then find the period of motion of its wings. Can you make predictions about how fast a bird will flap its wings based on the size of its wings?

  Extend this project by trying to find out what musical note a hummingbird hums. How about mosquitoes—can you find out their annoying frequency? Next look up the wing-flap rates of honeybees and bumblebees. Graph these data compared to body mass. Are these two factors related?

- When armies cross a bridge, the soldiers don't march in step. Is there a reason marching in step might be a problem? Design an experiment to investigate this.

- When you carry a pan of water across a room, the water sometimes sloshes back and forth. Does its motion have a characteristic frequency? Design an experiment to find out.

  After you have done this once, try other types of containers, such as an aquarium, and other depths of water. You may even be able to do this experiment in a sink or a bathtub. Would a swimming pool be too big? Try to predict the natural frequency of oscillation of very big bodies of water, such as Hudson Bay in Canada, the Sea of Japan, or the Caribbean Sea.

COMPARING SOUNDS

A trombone, a guitar, and a flute sound very different to us—even if they are all playing the same note. To produce the same note, all three instruments must vibrate at the same frequency. We hear different sounds because the instruments don't vibrate at the same frequency. The strength of the other frequencies determines the quality of the sound.

Have you ever noticed that people do not sound the same over the phone and in person? Why does a live concert sound different from a recorded one? When you hear a recording of your voice, does it sound strange? To learn more about how missing frequencies can affect quality of sound, try the following project. You may want to ask your school's music teacher to help you.

GUITAR OSCILLATIONS

What You Need	
Acoustic guitar	Guitar pick
Tabletop	Friend

Place the guitar on a table or flat surface that will not scratch the back of the guitar. Pluck a string with your finger and listen to the *pitch*. Pluck the other strings and listen to their pitches. What differences do you hear?

Place a finger firmly on a string near one of the frets—the bands that go across the neck—and then pluck the string with your other hand. How has the pitch changed? Pluck the string with your finger in different spots, such as on the middle of the string, where it is normally plucked, and right next to the bridge (where the string is attached). What differences do you hear? Which positions seem to amplify the higher pitches? You could use a sound probe connected to a computer or any one of a number of shareware computer programs to "see" these sounds.

Play a *musical scale* on the lowest-sounding string. Notice how the last note sounds. Then pluck the string while holding your finger over the fret you used to play the last note. Quickly remove your finger. You have just played what is known as the second harmonic. How does this note sound compared to the first one you played? Is the pitch the same? Does it sound the same? Ask a friend to press firmly on the front of the guitar. Pluck the string. Do the notes sound different? If so, why?

Now use a pick to produce sounds on the guitar. Is the quality of the sound like any other sound you produced in this experiment?

What other sounds can you produce with the guitar? Why do they sound different? Can you see these differences on the computer screen? The differences in the quality of the pitches are related to the strength of the harmonics that are played. The tinny sounds emphasize higher frequencies or higher harmonics. The rich tones emphasize lower frequencies.

Doing More
- Compare the way different shapes and types of guitars sound. Why do you think they sound different? Expensive guitars generally sound better than inexpensive ones. Why?

- Listen to various instruments in an orchestra. Try to relate the quality of their sounds to what the instruments are made from and how they are played.

- Use a brass instrument to find out how pitch and tone change under different conditions. What happens when a mute or your hand is placed in the open end of a trumpet or trombone? Why does this change occur? What happens when the mute is pushed farther into the bell of the instrument?

- Ask to borrow an oscilloscope from your school's science lab. Attach it to a microphone and study the wave patterns of different instruments and the voices of different people. (You might be able to use your home computer to do the same thing.) Compare your friends' speaking voices to their singing voices. What happens when they pinch their noses and then speak? Ask a friend to speak directly into the microphone and then go home and call you on the telephone. Does your friend's voice have a different pattern when it comes over the phone?

- Use a graphic calculator or a computer program, such as *Graphing Calculator*, to plot a sine wave on the screen. (If you aren't sure what a sine wave is, ask a math teacher for help.) Then change your program so you can plot the sum of two or more sine waves with different frequencies. This allows you to display harmonics on the screen. Harmonics are integer multiples of the first frequency, so if you make a wave with a first frequency of 1 cycle/sec, the harmonics would be 2 cycles/sec, 3 cycles/sec, 4 cycles/sec, and so on. Try changing the amplitude, or the maximum size, of the harmonics. How does it change the resulting wave?

- Now use a sound modifying program on a computer (many shareware and freeware programs are available from Internet locations, such as *http://www.download.com*) and play with the shape of the sound wave. How does this change the sound? Can you make instrument sounds that nobody has ever created before? If you want to use this as a science fair project, don't forget to keep notes, take screen shots of your wave forms, and frequently save your work. Remember to save the files with distinct names so you can show the orderly progression of experimentation by which you arrived at your new sound.

REGULATING ELECTRIC CURRENT

Have you ever wondered how electricity can do so many different types of jobs? It can be used to give us light, measure temperature, make a telephone ring, or change the volume of a stereo. A stereo sends an alternating electric current to the speakers, and they vibrate to make music. Electricity is a wonderful thing, but sometimes we need to turn it off. After all, there is a no reason to use lamps on a sunny day. And what would be the point of keeping a washing machine or a dishwasher on all the time?

That's why the amount of electricity flowing through a device can be controlled with switches. Many switches take advantage of Ohm's law.

$$\text{current (in amps)} = \frac{\text{voltage (in volts)}}{\text{resistance (in ohms)}}$$

The higher the resistance, the lower the current.

The following project will help you understand how switches work and what electrical resistance is. Before you do the project, you will need an ammeter to measure current. You could borrow one from your school, buy one at a hardware store or an electronics store, or build one using the directions provided in Appendix 2. Make sure that the ammeter can easily measure a current of 1 amp. If the ammeter is designed to measure much larger cur-

Have you ever wondered why you can turn off all the
lights in a room with a single switch on the wall?

rents, it will be difficult to see the differences in current that occur during this experiment. If the ammeter is designed to measure much smaller currents, you may burn it out during this experiment.

A LOOK AT RESISTORS

What You Need	
Ammeter	Insulated wire
Tape	Switch
Two 1.5-volt batteries	Ten 10-ohm resistors

Create a circuit in which current flows from one battery through the ammeter, through a 10-ohm resistor, through the switch, and back to the battery. See Figure 12. Make sure that the switch is in the "off," or open, position so that no current will flow while you are hooking up your equipment.

When you have everything set up correctly, test it by briefly closing the switch or turning it to the "on" position. If the needle on the ammeter goes past the end of the scale, open the switch immediately or you may burn out your meter. Follow this procedure every time you change the circuit. If you built your own ammeter using the instructions in Appendix 2, you don't have to worry about burning out your meter.

If you had to open your switch because too much current was flowing, add a few more resistors so the current must flow through them all to get around the circuit. Test the circuit again. *Caution: If your battery begins to get hot, stop your project immediately.*

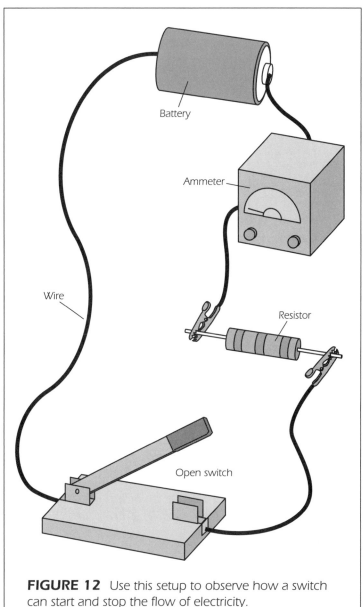

Battery

Ammeter

Wire

Resistor

Open switch

FIGURE 12 Use this setup to observe how a switch can start and stop the flow of electricity.

What happens to the circuit's resistance when the switch is closed or opened? What happens if you add a few more resistors to the circuit? Does the current in your ammeter change? What happens when you double the resistance of the circuit by adding another resistor to the series? What happens if you set up a circuit with two resistors in parallel? What happens when you use two batteries?

Doing More
- Use a rheostat, or variable resistor, with a resistance of 10 to 100 ohms in a circuit. How does it affect the current in your circuit. *Caution: Be careful not to send too much current through your ammeter.*

- Get a thermistor with a resistance in the 10-ohm range and see how its resistance changes as the temperature changes. How could you turn a thermistor into a thermometer?

- Place a resistor in ice water and measure how much current flows through it. Then place it in boiling water and check the current flow. What differences do you observe? What happens at other temperatures?

- Use an ammeter, a resistor, and a battery to find the resistance of various objects. Possibilities include metals, wood, and glass. Record your results. *Caution: To make sure that you do not blow out your ammeter, always make your first connection to a new material very brief.*

- If you are familiar with how transistors work, find how the resistance of the transistor varies with the gate, or base, voltage. Different transistors behave differently, so you may want to test different ones.

HOW A GENERATOR WORKS

Most of the electricity we use is generated by coils of wire and magnets. In large power-generating plants, magnets are turned near coils of wire. As the *magnetic fields* in the coils of wire change, an electric current is generated.

The generators in this power plant in Pennsylvania convert energy from flowing water into a form that can be used to light your home at night.

Because the magnetic fields keep changing back and forth, the current alternates so the charges vibrate back and forth.

According to Lenz's law, current flows so as to oppose a change in magnetic field in a loop of wire. To get a better understanding of this law, you can build a generator and use it to conduct some experiments.

BUILDING A GENERATOR

What You Need	
3-m piece of thin, insulated wire	Tabletop
	Wire clothes hanger
Ammeter	Tape
Magnet	

Wrap the middle 1-m section of the wire into a loop about 3 cm in diameter. This leaves two 1-m-long sections of wire at each end. Remove the insulation from the ends of the wire and connect them to the ammeter. Place the magnet on a table.

Quickly move the coil of wire toward the magnet. Observe your ammeter. What happens? Record your results. Hold the coil stationary near the magnet. What happens to the ammeter?*

Now unwind the top of the clothes hanger. Push a short piece of clothes-hanger wire through the coil so you can spin the coil by rolling the wire in your fingers. Tape

* If you are using an ammeter from a science lab, you may find that sometimes the needle moves the "wrong way." This means current is flowing in the opposite direction from the way it flows when the ammeter moves the "right way."

the wire in place. Move the coil near the magnet and see if you can make a current flow by spinning the coil between your fingers. What do you observe?

Now tape another piece of clothes-hanger wire to the magnet so you can spin the magnet by rolling the wire in your fingers. Lay the coil of wire flat on the table, move the magnet near it, and turn the magnet. What happens as you do this? Do your results change if you move the magnet faster or slower? Does it matter how close the magnet is to the coil?

What other ways can you make current flow through the coil of wire? What seems to be the underlying principle that causes current to flow? Does Lenz's law explain your results?

Doing More
- Design and build a windmill or waterwheel that generates a current. To do this, the model must turn a coil of wire in a magnetic field.

- Design and build a spark generator. To do this, develop a setup that runs current through a coil of wire that has many twists and turns. When a wire connected to the power source is suddenly removed, you will produce a spark. *Caution: Remove all paper and other flammable materials away from your work area.* Where does the spark appear? Can you think of any way to use this device to build a charcoal-fire starter? Do built-in barbecue lighters work this way?

WHAT IS A MAGNETIC FIELD?
Because magnetic fields affect the movement of charged particles, it is important for scientists to understand the shape of the magnetic field around an object. How do sci-

entists "see" the shape of a magnetic field? How do they figure out how two magnetic fields interact with one another? Does the field of an electromagnet—a magnet made from coils of wire that carry an electric current—look any different from that of a permanent magnet?

Magnetic fields around magnets and coils of wire are interesting to observe. The following project will help you learn more about magnetic fields.

"SEEING" MAGNETIC FIELDS

What You Need	
Notebook paper	Magnets of different shapes
Tape	
Tabletop	Pencil
	2 m long thin wire
Small compass	Flashlight battery

Tape a piece of paper to the table and place a bar magnet on top of it. Trace the shape of the magnet on the paper so you will have a permanent record of its position. Next place the compass on the paper. When the compass needle stops moving, draw an arrow on the paper to indicate the direction in which the compass needle points. Move the compass to other positions on the paper. For each position, draw an arrow to indicate which way the compass needle points.

Now move the compass far away from the magnet. Where does the compass needle point? It should point to magnetic north. Slowly move the compass toward the magnet. Does the needle change direction? Your diagram of the magnetic field of the magnet is really the result of the magnet's magnetic field as well as Earth's magnetic field.

Repeat the experiment using a magnet with a different shape. What differences do you expect in the shape of the field? Do your results match your hypothesis?

Using the thin wire, make a coil of wire 3 cm in diameter. Tape the coil to the paper so that it is in the vertical plane, that is, standing on edge. Remove the insulation on the ends of the wire and attach the coil to a battery with tape. Using the compass, find the magnetic field around this electromagnet. *Caution: If the battery gets hot, disconnect it immediately.*

Doing More

- Place two different types of magnets next to one another. Use a compass to find the combined magnetic field. Are you surprised by the shape? How does one magnet affect the magnetic field of another magnet?

- Sometimes scientists want to create a uniform magnetic field. Can you use two or more magnets to form such a field?

- Find the magnetic fields of a number of kitchen appliances or toys with magnets in them. Can you figure out how the magnets must be oriented to create the fields you "see"?

THE POWER OF ELECTROMAGNETS

Electromagnets are often more useful than permanent magnets because they can be turned on and off. Electromagnets are used in buzzers, disk drives, VCRs, and hundreds of other devices.

In the following project, you will make an electromagnet that can be switched on and off. As you experiment with the electromagnet, observe what happens when you make and break the connection going to the coil of wire. How fast does the field change as you turn the current on and off?

EXPERIMENTING WITH AN ELECTROMAGNET

What You Need	
5-m thin, insulated wire	Switch
10 cm of copper or aluminum tubing, 0.6 cm in diameter	Iron nail that fits into the tubing
	Assorted iron nails
1.5-volt battery	Wooden blocks
Tape	2-cm-wide steel strips

Remove 1 cm of insulation from each end of the wire. Create a wire coil by wrapping the wire around the entire length of the tubing. Be sure to leave about 20 cm of the wire unwrapped. This part of the wire will be attached to the switch. When you reach the end of the tubing, add a second layer of wrapped wire. Continue to do this until about 20 cm of wire is left unwrapped. This part of the wire will be attached to the battery. After you have made your coil, add a layer of tape on top so the coil doesn't unwind.

Tape one end of the wire to the switch and the other end to one terminal of the battery. Connect the other side of the switch to the battery. *Caution: Make sure the switch is in the "off," or open position so no current flows as you make the connections.*

Now put a few nails on the table and close the switch of your electromagnet. How many nails can you pick up with your coil of wire? Don't leave the battery connected too long—if you do, it will go dead. ***Caution: If the battery gets hot, disconnect it immediately.***

Insert a nail into one end of the tubing, and tape it in place. Reconnect the wire coil to the battery and the switch. What happens?

Doing More

- Can you figure out a way to use your coil to make a switch that will turn a flashlight bulb on and off?

- Sprinkle iron filings on a sheet of paper and then slowly move the coil of wire across the paper as you turn the current on and off. What happens to the filings? This is similar to what happens to the magnetic particles in magnetic tapes used in tape recorders, disk drives, and VCRs. What happens when you change the speed of motion or the strength of the magnet?

- Make a buzzer that operates using a coil of wire and a power source. Design it so that when current goes through the coil, it makes the clapper of the buzzer move toward the coil. However, as the clapper moves toward the coil, it disconnects the power source. Now, with no current, the clapper isn't attracted to the coil. The clapper moves away from the magnet, the connection is made again, current flows, and the process repeats. What factors affect the frequency at which an electric buzzer rings? How can you change the frequency of the buzzer?

- Design and build an electric door lock. How would you design the lock so you can still open it if the battery goes dead?

APPENDIX 1

SCIENCE FAIRS

Entering a project in a science fair can be very reward-ing. When you know that you must make a presen-tation, you are forced to look at your project critically and to ask questions about your data and conclusions. After all, it can be embarrassing when someone points out a flaw in your reasoning or asks a question that you cannot answer. If you don't analyze your data thoroughly, you will not win a prize.

A science fair project is judged on the basis of origi-nality, presentation, and scientific content. Other people may have done projects similar to yours in the past, but yours should have a new viewpoint or a better method for collecting data. You must also show that you understand what you did and show that your conclusions are based on sound principles and good data.

Your project will be viewed by many people, and you have to make sure it answers the questions students,

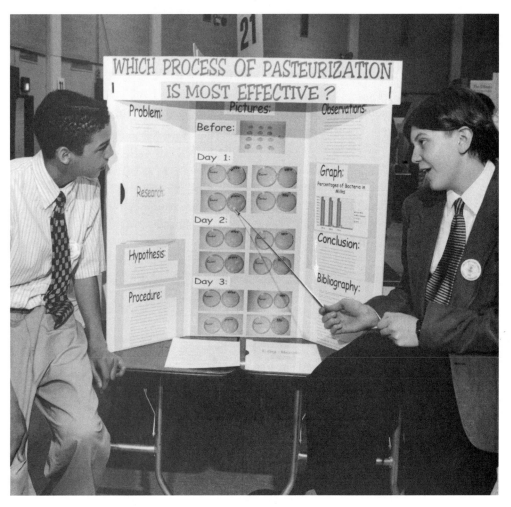

This student has worked hard on his science fair project. Do you think he will win a prize?

teachers, parents, and judges may ask. You must state clearly what you did, show your data in a logical manner, and indicate how you reached your conclusions. Sometimes preparing for a science fair seems like a lot of work, but in the end it helps you to learn more from your project.

THE PRESENTATION

Prizewinning science fair projects never consist of just a paper. You need to have something to catch the judges' attention. Create a clear, colorful presentation. If your display includes something that viewers can do, it will be a hit.

Using computer programs, such as *PowerPoint* or *ClarisWorks* (*AppleWorks*), can help make your presentation more organized and interesting. These programs will allow you to show your arguments point by point, create clear tables and graphs, and include sound and animation. It is also possible to have the presentation run automatically and continuously.

If you do this, make sure someone is always watching the computer equipment so it doesn't get damaged or stolen. You also need a large computer screen so more than one person can see the presentation at a time.

DESIGNING AND DOING THE PROJECT

Here is the process you should follow as you develop and conduct your project.

1. Choose a topic that interests you.

2. Do some research to come up with a project idea.

3. Think of an original hypothesis.

4. Design an experiment to test your hypothesis.

5. Conduct the experiment.

6. Organize your data in tables and graphs. Look for any results that seem strange or inconsistent.

7. Make sure that your conclusions are supported by your data. If there are other ways to interpret your data, state them and show why your interpretation makes more sense.

8. Ask a friend, family member, or teacher to look at your data? Does the person have trouble understanding your graphs or the way you have explained your data. If he or she is confused, try to make your presentation clearer.

9. Write a report that consists of

   • a title page with the name of your project, your name, the name of your school, your address, and the date

   • an acknowledgments section in which you thank the people who helped you or let you borrow equipment

   • a table of contents

   • a statement of purpose in which you describe what you were trying to show

   • an abstract that allows readers to quickly find out what you did and what you found. Here's an example.

MOTION ON ROTATING PLATFORMS

A study was done on a rotating platform to investigate the path of a rolling ball relative to the platform. Because the ball rolls, the path will not be the same as if the ball were just moving across a smooth surface. Hollow and solid balls of different sizes were used. It was shown that the path taken by the balls was similar to the one predicted by a computer model.

- a background section that contains the information you found at a library or on the Internet as well as a basic explanation of relevant scientific principles

- a procedure that explains how you conducted the experiment. This section should include a description of the apparatus, including photographs and drawings if possible.

- a results section that shows your data in a clear way. Graphs and tables may help present the information effectively.

- a conclusion that describes what you found when you analyzed your data

- a bibliography that lists books, articles, and other sources you used.

BUILDING AN AMMETER

What You Need	
2-m piece of thin insulated wire Compass	Tape Dry-cell battery

Wind the wire into a coil just large enough to put the compass inside. Wrap tape around the coil so it doesn't uncoil and lose its shape. Leave straight ends of the wire about 10 cm long so that you can attach it to a battery or other wires. Remove the insulation from the last 1 cm on each end to give good conductivity.

Place the compass inside the wire. The coil should be pointed north-south—parallel to the compass needle. You may have to build a cardboard stand so the coil will stay in this position.

Attach one wire to one end of the battery with tape and briefly touch the other wire to the other end of the battery. What happens? Try switching wires on the battery. What happens? The meter you have just built is not as good as ones used in most science labs, but it will allow you to see changes in current.

GLOSSARY

acceleration—the rate of change of velocity per unit of time

alternating current—current that periodically switches direction

angular acceleration—the rate of change of angular velocity or rotation rate

angular velocity—rate of rotation; usually expressed in radians or degrees per second

buoyancy—a property of matter that allows a substance to float

calorie—the amount of heat needed to raise the temperature of 1 gram of water 1°C; 1 calorie equals 4.185 joules

centripetal acceleration—acceleration toward the center of a circle

coefficient of friction—the ratio of frictional force to the force between the surfaces

elastic collision—a collision in which objects rebound from each other without the loss of kinetic energy

equilibrium position—the state in which all forces are balanced

force—the physical quantity that can affect the motion of an object (a push or pull)

frequency—the number of vibrations, oscillations, or cycles per unit time

friction—a force that opposes motion between two surfaces as one slips over the other

heat—thermal energy in the process of being added to or removed from objects. Objects with a lot of heat have a lot of atoms moving quickly. Heat is not the same as temperature.

hypothesis—a plausible solution to a problem; a guess you're going to test in an experiment to verify or discard as a solution

inelastic collision—a collision in which the colliding objects stick together after impact, such as your shoe and a piece of bubble gum, unlike your shoe and a soccer ball (see elastic collision)

kinetic energy—energy possessed by an object because it is moving (see potential energy)

magnetic field—a region in which a magnet feels a force. If it moves a compass needle, it's a magnetic field.

mass—a measure of the amount of material; a fundamental physical quantity. Mass is not the same as weight.

mechanics—the study of motion and energy

moment of inertia—related to the mass of an object and how far it is from the axis of rotation

momentum—the product of the mass and the velocity of a moving body

musical scale—the notes that make up an octave

newton—the unit of force in the metric system; a derived unit having the dimensions of $kg \cdot m/sec^2$. The force required to accelerate a 1-kilogram mass at a rate of 1 meter per second each second. The English unit of force is the pound, equal to about 4.45 newtons.

period—the time for one complete cycle, vibration, revolution, or oscillation (as in a pendulum)

permeability——the ability of molecules to migrate into another area

pitch—a sound caused by a particular frequency

potential energy—energy that is the result of the position of an object in a gravitational, magnetic, or electric field

precession—the rotation of a spinning object about one axis when it is turned about another axis

pressure—force per area

quantitative—an observation that measures how much of something, compared to a known standard. For example, 3.68 meters in length or brighter than a candle flame.

scientific method—the process scientists use to test and evaluate an idea

solubility—he ability of a substance to dissolve in another material

surface tension—the force between molecules at the surface of a liquid

tangent—parallel to the circumference of a circle at a fixed point

torque—the product of a force times the distance away from the pivot point or axis of rotation; parallel to the circumference of a circle at a fixed point. In mathematics, the ratio of the length of the legs of a right triangle.

velocity—the speed in a particular direction

work—a force exerted over a certain distance. It is a form of energy.

RESOURCES

BOOKS

Adams, Richard, and Robert Gardner. *Ideas for Science Projects.* Danbury, CT: Franklin Watts, 1997.

_____. *More Ideas for Science Projects.* Danbury, CT: Franklin Watts, 1998.

Asimov, Isaac. *Understanding Physics* (vols. 1, 2, & 3). New York: Dorset Press, 1988.

Berg, Richard and David G. Stone. *Physics of Sound.* Englewood Cliffs, NJ: Prentice-Hall, 1994.

Bohren, Craig. *What Light through Yonder Window Breaks.* New York: John Wiley & Sons, 1991.

Crane, Richard. *How Things Work.* College Park, MD: American Association of Physics Teachers, 1992.

Ehrlich, Robert. *Turning the World Inside Out and 174 Other Simple Physics Demonstrations.* Princeton, NJ: Princeton University Press, 1990.

Falk, David, Dieter Brill, and David Stork. *Seeing the Light.* New York: John Wiley & Sons, 1986.

Graf, Rudolf. *Safe and Simple Electrical Experiments.* New York: Dover, 1964.

Herbert, Don. *Mr. Wizard's Experiments for Young Scientists.* New York: Doubleday, 1959.

Hewitt, Paul. *Conceptual Physics*. New York: Scott, Foresman & Co., 1997.

Hosking, Wayne. *Flights of Imagination*. Washington, D.C.: National Science Teachers Association, 1987.

Hutchins, Carleen. *The Physics of Music*. San Francisco: W. H. Freeman and Co., 1978.

Macaulay, David. *The Way Things Work*. New York: Houghton Mifflin, 1988.

Pierce, John. *The Science of Musical Sound*. New York: W. H. Freeman, 1992.

Sarquis, Jerry L., Mickey Sarquis, and John P. Williams. *Teaching Physics with TOYS*. New York: Tab Books, 1995.

Scott, John. *Electricity, Electronics and You*. Portland, Maine: J. Weston Walch, 1981.

Strongin, Herb. *Science on a Shoestring*. Reading, MA: Addison-Wesley Publishing Co., 1991.

WEB SITES

About Temperature
http://www.unidata.ucar.edu/staff/blynds/tmp.html
This site features a very good discussion of thermodynamics and includes graphics.

Ask Science Questions
http://www-hpcc.astro.washington.edu/scied/sciask.html
A good place for help with projects.

Glenbrook High School "The Project Corner"
http://www.glenbrook.k12.il.us/gbssci/phys/projects/proj.html

This site has lots of project ideas done by students at this high school.

Project Physics
http://www.amersol.edu.pe/_kacres/project.html
Plenty of ideas for physics projects.

Science World Wide Web Resources
http://www.esd105.wednet.edu/science.html
This site has links to many interesting home pages.

The Tech Museum of Innovation
http://www.thetech.org/hyper/
This site has links to ongoing physics projects.

INDEX

(Italicized page numbers indicate illustrations.)

ABOUT THE AUTHORS

Richard C. Adams teaches high school physics, chemistry, computers, photography, world history, and foreign languages at Pleasant Hill High School in Pleasant Hill, Oregon and is the Webmaster for his school district. He also teaches chemistry at Marylhurst University near Portland, Oregon. He holds a B.A. in chemistry from California State University, Los Angeles, and an M.A. in physics, biology, and computer science from the University of Oregon. Mr. Adams has also authored *Science with Computers*, and coauthored *Ideas for Science Projects, More Ideas for Science Projects*, and *Science Projects in Energy* with Robert Gardner, and *Engineering Projects for Young Scientists* with Peter Goodwin, all for Franklin Watts. His hobbies include photography, calligraphy, science fiction, and atrocious puns. He lives with his wife, Stephanie, in houses in Eugene and Florence, Oregon. His son and daughter are away at college.

Peter H. Goodwin teaches high school physics and astronomy and chairs the science department at the Kent School in Kent, Connecticut. He holds a B.A. in physics from Middlebury College in Middlebury, Vermont, and an M.A. in education from Trinity College in Hartford, Connecticut. Mr. Goodwin has also coauthored *Engineering Projects for Young Scientists* for Franklin Watts. His hobbies include photography, playing the guitar, canoeing, cross-country skiing, orienteering, and gardening in his solar greenhouse. He lives with his wife, Susan, and two sons in a house he built himself.